Sleep 2.1 Manual

"If you put a million monkeys at a million keyboards, one of them will eventually write a Java program. The rest of them will write Perl programs." -- Anonymous

Raphael Mudge

Sleep 2.1 Manual
Revision: 06.02.08

Table of Contents

Introduction

I. What is Sleep?

The java world currently has Jacl for TCL, Jython for Python, and JRuby for Ruby. One offering is missing from this bunch: what Java offering exists for the Perl hackers of the world?

Sleep is a Java-based scripting language heavily inspired by Perl. Sleep started out as a weekend long hack fest in April 2002. When nothing like Perl was available to build a scriptable Internet Relay Chat client, I set out to build the scripting language I wanted.

Go ahead and download jIRCii to see what Sleep can do. http://jircii.dashnine.org/

Sleep has evolved beyond its beginnings as a scripting engine for a chat program. Today Sleep primitives include strings, doubles, integers, and containers for holding objects and functions. Arrays and hashes can combine these primitives into complex data structures. Closures that respond to "messages" act as a flexible means of abstraction. Also The entire Java API is accessible as if the Java Objects were functions that respond to "messages".

Sleep Website

It is about 11:30pm on a Friday night and I would love to know where I can get some sleep. All puns aside, the latest version of Sleep is always available at the Sleep homepage:

http://sleep.dashnine.org/

You will find documentation, script examples, articles, and extensions at the Sleep homepage.

How to receive support

Most sleep discussion takes place on a google group. Through this group you can see what is on the horizon with Sleep and comment on open ideas. This is also a great place to report bugs and receive support.

http://groups.google.com/group/sleep-developers/

If you prefer to chat with a living person, you may find me and some Sleep hackers on internet relay chat (IRC). We are in the **#jIRCii** channel on the EFNet IRC network. A list of EFNet servers is available at http://www.efnet.org/

Sleep Snippets Blog

O'Reilly and Associates has a successful series of books on technology hacks. These books consist of about 100 stand-alone tips and code snippets around a core subject. In this spirit Sleep has the Sleep Snippets Weblog. Each new snipppet (with explanation) shows off cool Sleep capabilities.

http://jroller.com/page/sleepsnip

II. Manual Conventions

This manual consists of two sections. The first section is a tutorial on the Sleep language. This section is small on purpose. Read it to get a good grounding in the terminology, idioms, and features of the Sleep language. The second section is a man-page style reference on the standard Sleep library. This reference includes descriptions of each parameter, example code, and related topics.

The following conventions exist throughout this manual.

A monospaced font signals source code.

```
println("hello world");
```

Italicized text refers to variable names.

$variable, @array, %hash.

This guide displays function names in a monospaced font.

`&foo`

Examples will occasionally show input or user originated commands. A strong typeface marks this.

```
java -jar sleep.jar
```

Program output is below:

> I am some output

This manual also highlights frequently asked questions.

> **What are these boxes?**
>
> This is a frequently asked questions box. These point out questions folks have asked in the past.

III. Acknowledgements

I'll keep this list short and sweet. I just want to quickly acknowledge some of the folks whose input has shaped Sleep. I'm still doing this project for the fun of it but its good to know these guys are out there. I'd like to thank Andreas Ravnestad for his work on Slumber. Andreas and Serge Baranov both deserve thanks for their contributions to jIRCii in the past. The jIRCii community put up with a very rough scripting language a few years ago. To that end I owe a thanks to phos, mexis, ceelow, tijiez, neuken, [rza], blue-elf, drakx, and all the others who put their creativity and enthusiasm into writing Sleep scripts for jIRCii. Thanks for finding the issues so others don't have to. I'd also like to thank Kurt von

Finck (mneptok) for his support and advocacy. Marty Sheppard deserves mad greets. He is one of the drivers throwing Sleep at real projects. His work and input has had quite an influence on Sleep. I also want to say thanks to skape, shane, ratdog, brian, and the rest of the hick.org crew. Hick hosted the Sleep and jIRCii sites for the first several years of their existence. Thanks to Brandon Mumby for providing me a place to run my experimental Sleep webserver. This "experimental" server is currently hosting the jIRCii and Sleep websites. Also I'll thank those of you who come out of nowhere emailing me oddball questions about Sleep in weird contexts. Thanks for keeping me amused.

1. Getting Started

1.1 Stand-alone Scripts

Sleep scripts run stand-alone from the command line using sleep.jar as the interpreter.

The traditional first script is usually the famous Hello World program. As I am a fan of tradition your first Sleep script will be a Hello World script as well.

To run the following script: type the source code into a text editor, save it as hello.sl, and then run it by typing: **java -jar sleep.jar hello.sl**

```
println("Hello World");
```

Hello World

Congratulations! You have written and ran your first Sleep script.

Command Line Arguments

Scripts run from the command line can receive arguments. Sleep stores arguments in the variable *@ARGV*. For example the following sleep script copies files. The source file is *@ARGV[0]* and the destination file is *@ARGV[1]*.

```
# cp.sl [original file] [new file]

$in = openf(@ARGV[0]);
```

```
$data = readb($in, -1);

$out = openf(">" . @ARGV[1]);
writeb($out, $data);

closef($in);
closef($out);
```

```
$ java -jar sleep.jar cp.sl hello.sl hello.bak
$ cat hello.bak
println("Hello World");
```

The *$__SCRIPT__* variable contains the name of the current script.

Command Line Options

Sleep accepts many command line arguments.

```
$ java -jar sleep.jar --help
Sleep 2.1 (20080515)
Usage: java [properties] -jar sleep.jar [options] [-|file|expression]
 properties:
  -Dsleep.assert=<true|false>
  -Dsleep.classpath=<path to locate 3rd party jars from>
  -Dsleep.debug=<debug level>
  -Dsleep.taint=<true|false>
 options:
  -a --ast      display the abstract syntax tree of the specified script
  -c --check    check the syntax of the specified file
  -e --eval     evaluate a script as specified on command line
  -h --help     display this help message
  -p --profile  collect and display runtime profile statistics
  -t --time     display total script runtime
  -v --version  display version information
  -x --expr     evaluate an expression as specified on the command line
 file:
  specify a '-' to read script from STDIN
```

Java passes the *[properties]* directly to Sleep. These properties are available from the `&systemProperties` function.

The *sleep.assert* property enables or disables assertions. This manual discusses assertions in 3.4 Assertions.

The *sleep.classpath* property specifies where Sleep should look for 3rd party jar files loaded with `import [path] from: [jar file]` and `&use`. Use a semicolon or colon between entries to specify more than one path. Chapter 7.1 Object Expressions: 3rd-party Jars discusses the `import from` ability in detail.

The *sleep.debug* property specifies the debug level to run the script with. This manual sprinkles script debugging topics throughout its pages.

The *sleep.taint* property enables or disables taint mode. When enabled, taint mode marks all data from external sources as tainted. Some Sleep functions do not accept tainted data. 6.1 Object Expressions: Taint Mode and Objects and 9.3 Sleep Integration: Taint Mode discuss this security feature in detail.

The Sleep console runs when there is no script file.

Can I start Sleep scripts with jrunscript?

Java 1.6 includes a new programming interface to allow interchangeable use of different script engines. Sleep 2.1 supports this interface and yes you can launch Sleep scripts with jrunscript. Make sure sleep.jar is in your classpath for the following to work:

```
$ jrunscript -l sleep -f hello.sl
```

@ARGV and *$__SCRIPT__* are available to scripts run through jrunscript.

1.2 The Sleep Console

The Sleep console is an environment that runs Sleep code interactively. You will know you are in the Sleep console when you see the following:

```
$ java -jar sleep.jar
>> Welcome to the Sleep scripting language
>
```

Help within the Console

The `help` command is available for getting help. Simply type `help` *command name* to receive information about a command. The help command by itself simply lists the available commands.

Evaluate an Expression

To evaluate an expression using the Sleep console use the `x` command.

```
> x 3 + 4
7
> x split(" ", "Hello World")
@('Hello', 'World')
> x [Math PI]
3.141592653589793
```

To evaluate a predicate expression (an if condition) use the ? command.

```
> ? 3 eq "3"
true
> ? 3 eq 3.0
false
> ? (3 == 3) && ($x is $null || 3 == 4)
true
```

Interact Mode

You can type any amount of Sleep code with interactive mode. Launch interactive mode with the `interact` command. Place a period on a line by itself once the code is ready for evaluation.

```
> interact
>> Welcome to interactive mode.
Type your code and then '.' on a line by itself to execute the code.
Type Ctrl+D or 'done' on a line by itself to leave interactive mode.

println("Hello World");
.
Hello World

$x = 4 * atan2(1, 1);
println($x);
.
3.141592653589793

if ($x == [Math PI])
{
  println("We have an accurate PI value!!");
}
.
We have an accurate PI value!!

done
>
```

To leave interactive mode press Ctrl+D or type `done` on a line by itself.

Abstract Syntax Trees

The Sleep parser transforms code into an abstract syntax tree. Sleep uses this form to interpret your script. To view an abstract syntax tree for a script use the `tree` *script name* command. The `tree` command by itself shows the abstract syntax tree of the most recent script.

```
> tree
[Decide]:
 [Condition]:
   [Predicate]: name->==  negated->false
     [Setup]:
       [Get Item]: $x
       [Create Frame]
       [Object Access]: class java.lang.Math#PI
 [If true]:
   [Create Frame]
   [Parsed Literal]  null
     [Element]: We have an accurate PI value!!
   [Function Call]: &println
 [If False]:
```

Debugging with the Console

Set the script debug level with the `debug` *level* command. Once set all script snippets run with the debug level. For example level 8 enables function call tracing.

```
> debug 8
Default debug level set
> load hello.sl
hello.sl loaded successfully.
Hello World
Trace: &println('Hello World') at line eval:1
```

2. Scalars

2.1 Scalar Expressions

Scalars are Sleep's universal data container. This chapter will cover how to assign and work with scalars. Later we will walk through some of the various types of scalars you will face while using Sleep.

A variable is a temporary location in memory to store a value. Sleep variables are scalars. Scalars can be strings, numbers, or even a reference to a Java object.

Scalar variable names always begin with the dollar sign.

> **Why do variable names have to begin with anything?**
>
> Because when I wrote the Sleep parser I was too lazy to write it correctly and make it recognize bare-word variables. That and Perl expects variable names to begin with a dollar sign as well. Happy?

Scalar variables (referred to as scalars from now on) hold several types of data. This chapter discusses the number and string types.

Assignment

Assign values to variables with the equal sign. For example:

```
$x = 3;
$y = $x;
```

This example places the integer 3 into the variable *$x* *$x* now contains the integer 3 until another statement assigns to it. The second line copies the value *$x* into *$y*. *$y* has the value 3.

There is no need to declare *$x* or *$y* before use. Sleep uses *$null* (the empty scalar) when a variable does not exist. Sleep discovers the type information of a value from the literal form. For example `"blah"` is a string scalar. In general a scalar is a container that holds a value. Assignment places a value into a scalar.

It is possible to declare variables before use. I recommend this practice as it helps with debugging. 5.2 Scalar Scope discusses variable declaration and debugging with strict mode.

How Values are Passed

The variable assignment process sometimes copies data and other times it copies a reference. Which of these occurs depends on the value's type.

Pass by value defines variable assignment that copies the assigned value. Changes made to a copy do not affect the original value. Sleep passes number and string values by value.

```
$x = 3;
$y = $x;
$x = 4;
```

In the example above *$x* is initially 3. Line 2 assigns *$y* a copy of *$x* which is 3. *$y* now has the value 3. The last line assigns the value 4 to *$x*. The assignment does not affect *$y* since it has a copy of the value 3.

Pass by reference is variable assignment that copies a reference to a value. Sleep uses references to share values between multiple scalars. Changes to one reference affect all scalars that reference the same data. This allows efficient use of computer memory for complex values. Sleep passes array, hash, and object values by reference.

```
# create a new java.lang.StringBuffer object
$a = [new StringBuffer: "hello"];

# assign a reference to the StringBuffer in $a to $b
$b = $a;

# append " world!" to the StringBuffer
[$b append: " world!"];
```

```
println($a);
println($b);
```

```
hello world!
hello world!
```

> **What does the pound sign represent?**
>
> Sleep uses the pound sign for comments. Sleep interprets anything following a pound sign up to the end of a line as a comment. The parser strips away comments. Comments are a tool to let you document your programs.

Getting ahead of ourselves, this example creates an object value and assigns it to *$a*. I then assign the object value in *$a* to *$b*. Sleep uses pass by reference since *$a* holds an object value. The next line appends the string `" world!"` to *$b*. The scalars *$a* and *$b* reference the same object. When the script prints out *$a* and *$b* the same result is shown for each.

I hope this discussion clarified variables (scalars), types, and means of passing them. In the future I will speak of scalars and types as the same entity. From now on read the phrase *string scalar* as: "A scalar container that holds a Sleep string value."

Expressions

You can assign the results of an operation to a scalar. An operation is an operator surrounded by two values. For example `2 + 3` is the + operator applied to the values `2` and `3`. Here are some valid operations:

```
$x = 5 + "1";
$x = 5 - $y;
$x = $x * $2;
$x = $z / 9.9;
$x = $1 % 3;  # modulus
$x = $1 ** 4; # exponentation
```

These operations work on numbers. There are operators for strings as well.

```
$x = "Ice" . "cream";
```

This example joins two strings with the string concatenation operator. *$x* has the string value: `"Icecream"`.

```
$x = "abc" x 3;
```

This example shows the string multiplication operator. This operator repeats the left operand as set by the right operand. Here *$x* is `"abcabcabc"` or `"abc"` repeated 3 times.

Combine multiple operators to form an expression.

```
$z = 5 + 1 * 3;
```

This example is valid. The plus, minus, and period (string concatenation) have lower precedence than multiplication, division, and modulus. This expression is equal to:

```
$z = 5 + (1 * 3);
```

Parentheses define which expression to evaluate first.

```
$z = 3 * ($x % 3) - (ticks() / (10000 + 1));
```

Assignment Operations

Sleep supports a special assignment form called an assignment operator. An assignment operator combines operation on a scalar and assignment into a single step.

```
$x = 4;

$x += 3;
println($x);
```

```
7
```

`$x += 3` is the same as `$x = $x + 3`. Assignment operations are faster as they are less work for the Sleep interpreter. These are valid assignment operations: +=, -=, *=, /=, &=, |=, ^=, <<=, >>=, and .=.

Mandated Whitespace

Sleep scripts expect white space in expressions. Many languages allow you to get away with little white space. The following is valid in Perl:

```
$x=1+2;
```

```
Error: Syntax error at line 1
    $x=1+2
```

Sleep does not know what to do with the statement above and as you can see it reports a syntax error. Your scripts must use white space between operators and their operands.

```
$x = 1 + 2;
```

Think of this as a feature that forces reasonable coding habits.

> **Why is white space needed?**
>
> Sleep is an extensible language. Sleep extensions (bridges) provide all the operations such as addition and subtraction. The Sleep parser does not know about these operators when it is parsing your script. The only way it knows an operator is an operator is by the context.
>
> Out of guilt I did add a hack to make Sleep recognize the string concatenation operator (a period) with or without white space. When I was in a Perl hacking mind-set I kept receiving parser errors because of my lack of whitespace around this operator. When I added this hack, I was already placing whitespace into my string concatenation operations. I managed to get over it.

Scalar Types

Sleep has many value types. This section summarizes them.

String Scalars

A string is a sequence of characters also know as arbitrary text. Any value may convert to a string. The integer `3` is equal to the string `"3"`.

```
$var = "This is some arbitrary text";
println($var);
```

This is some arbitrary text

Numerical Scalars

Sleep has several number types. This chapter discusses them later.

```
$x = 3;   # integer
$y = 3.4; # double
$z = 45L; # long (64bit integer)
```

Arrays

Arrays are a scalar that contain multiple values. Arrays store their values in numerical order. You may recall an array value by position.

```
@foo = @("a", "b", "c");
$x = @foo[1] # $x is now "b"
```

Hash Scalars

Hashes hold multiple values as well. Hashes act like dictionaries. You can store and lookup values by keyword.

```
%bar = %(x => "x-ray", y => "yabboes");
$x = %bar["y"]; # $x is now "yabboes"
```

Object Scalars

Sleep scalars may refer to Java objects. The function `&openf` creates an object holding the file handle. Sleep's input and output functions know how to work with this handle object.

```
$handle = openf("hello.txt");

# call the readln function on the object scalar
# that references a file handle for hello.txt
$text = readln($handle);
```

You can also create Java objects through object expressions. Earlier you saw the pass by reference example create a `java.lang.StringBuffer` object. Chapter 7 covers this topic in-depth.

Function Scalars

Sleep functions are first class types. You can assign them to variables, pass them as parameters to functions, and all that other fun stuff. A function scalar is an object scalar that references a `sleep.bridges.SleepClosure` object.

The mysterious $null

$null is the null scalar. The null scalar is equal to nothingness. You cannot assign a value to *$null*.

$null is equal to the number `0`. As a string *$null* is equal to the empty string `""`. As an object *$null* is the same as the Java value `null`. Use the `is` predicate to check if a scalar is *$null*.

```
$ java -jar sleep.jar
>> Welcome to the Sleep scripting language
> ? $null eq ""
true
```

```
> ? $null is ""
false
> ? $null is 0
false
> ? $null is $null
true
```

Scalar Descriptions

Many of Sleep's built-in debugging and runtime warning messages provide a description of your data. Knowing scalar descriptions will help you decipher what Sleep is telling you about your program behavior. This table summarizes the descriptions that Sleep uses for each type:

Type	Example
String	`'some value'`
Integer	`3`
Long	`4L`
Double	`5.4`
Object	`...`
Array	`@(...)`
Hash	`%(...)`
Key/Value Pair	*key* `=>` *value*
Closure	`&closure[script.sl:3-5]#4`
Null Scalar	`$null`

Use the `&typeOf` function to find out the type of a scalar.

```
$long    = 4L;
$double  = 3.5;

$result  = $long + $double; # what is the result?

println("Type of result is: " . typeOf($result));
```

```
Type of result is: class sleep.engine.types.DoubleValue
```

2.2 Numbers

Sleep supports three types of scalars for numbers. Whole numbers such as `-1`, `0`, `1`, `2` ... `65536` are integer values. Double values have a decimal in them such as `3.0`, `1.1`, `0.55556`. This example assigns a double value to a scalar:

```
$Pi = 3.1415926535;
```

You can use the hexadecimal form to specify integers. A hexadecimal number begins with `0x`.

```
$var = 0xFF; # same as $var = 255
```

Sleep also supports octal literals. A number that begins with a leading zero is an octal number.

```
$oct = 077; # same as $var = 63
```

A long is a higher capacity integer. Integer scalars use 32 bits. Longs use 64. An integer can represent a whole number between `-2,147,483,648` to `+2,147,483,64`. A long has a larger capacity.

Add an `L` to the end of a number to declare a long. For example, `12345L` is a long scalar. The `L` accepts hex and octal literals as well.

Use `&formatNumber` and `&parseNumber` to format and parse numbers in other bases.

Increment and Decrement Operators

Sleep has a special operator for integer scalars. Instead of typing

```
$x = $x + 1;
```

You can use the increment operator on the scalar *$x*.

```
$x++;
```

The two are equivalent. `$x++` increments the value of *$x* and returns `$x + 1`. The decrement operator works similiarly except it subtracts rather than adds. `$x--` decrements the value of *$x* and returns `$x - 1`.

Useful Constants

The Java class library contains several numerical constants. Use an object expression to access them. PI is available as `[Math PI]` and E is available as `[Math E]`. These constructs return double scalars.

```
# show off mathematical constants.

$Pi = [Math PI];
println("Pi is $Pi");
```

```
$E  = [Math E];
println("E  is $E");
```

```
Pi is 3.141592653589793
E  is 2.718281828459045
```

This table shows the operators available for manipulating number scalars.

Operator	Description
*	multiplication
/	division
+	addition
-	subtraction
%	modulus; remainder operator
**	exponentation
<=>	numerical comparison

The multiplication and division operators have a higher precedence than all other operators. For bit twiddling Sleep provides the following operators:

Operator	Description
<<	left shift
>>	right shift
^	exclusive or
&	and
|	or
not(*$x*)	negates *$x*

Logical operators are only valid on scalar longs and ints. Sleep will do its best to convert other types to a fitting int value.

Conversion of Scalars

When performing a numerical operation or comparison on different types a conversion will occur. For example, Sleep will convert an operand to a double if the other operand is a double. The result of this operation is a double as well. A similar process occurs for longs. Integers have the lowest conversion priority.

Use casting functions to force a scalar to a certain type.

Function	Description
double(*$x*)	returns the value of *$x* as a double scalar
long(*$x*)	returns the value of *$x* as a long scalar
int(*$x*)	returns the value of *$x* as a int scalar

More sophisticated casting exists for the purpose of interacting with Java. Chapter 7 introduces these.

Time and Date Values

Sleep scripts can work with date and time values. Sleep stores date and time values as a long with the number of milliseconds since the epoch. Sleep's epoch is midnight, January 1st, 1970. Sleep uses this millisecond form instead of a string representation.

The `&formatDate` and `&parseDate` functions expect a datetime format string. `&formatDate` formats a date and time value into a string representation. The `&parseDate` creates a date and time value from a string representation and a datetime format.

A datetime format specifies a template of a date and time string representation. Sleep interprets unquoted letters from `'A'` to `'Z'` and `'a'` to `'z'` in the pattern as parts of a date or time template. Avoid this interpretation by surrounding text with single quotes. For example `'at'` represents the word at.

The following pattern letters are available (Java currently reserves other characters):

Letter	Description	Examples
G	Era designator	AD
y	Year	2004 ; 04
M	Month in year	October ; Oct ; 10
w	Week in year	27
W	Week in month	2
D	Day in year	127
d	Day in month	10
F	Day of week in month	2
E	Day in week	Monday ; Mon
a	Am/pm marker	PM
H	Hour in day (0-23)	0
k	Hour in day (1-24)	24
K	Hour in am/pm (0-11)	0
h	Hour in am/pm (1-12)	11
m	Minute in hour	34
s	Second in minute	52
S	Millisecond	745
z	Time zone	Eastern Standard Time ;EST ;GMT-04:00
Z	Time zone	-0400

Repeat pattern letters to specify the exact presentation. For example `'E'` is the day of week pattern letter. `'EEE'` refers to the short form of the day of the week such as Weds. `'EEEE'` refers to the long form such as Wednesday. Another example: `'yy'` will truncate the year to 2 digits.

The `&ticks` function returns the current time in milliseconds since the epoch. This example shows date formatting and parsing in action:

```
# lets do a little 'date' arithmetic

$event = "14/Oct/2006:12:24:00 -0500";
$a     = parseDate('dd/MMM/yyyy:kk:mm:ss Z', $event);

$now   = "2006.10.14 at 13:40:00 EDT";
$b     = parseDate("yyyy.MM.dd 'at' HH:mm:ss z", $now);

# keep in mind we are dealing with milliseconds
# i.e. 60 * 1000 = 1 minute
$diff = $b - $a;
println("event occured " . ($diff / 60000) . " minutes ago");

# subtract the difference from our "now" value
$when = $b - $diff;

println("event occured " . formatDate($when, "yyyy.MM.dd 'at' HH:mm:ss
z"));
```

event occured 16 minutes ago
event occured 2006.10.14 at 13:24:00 EDT

2.3 Strings

Sleep strings come in two varieties. Literals and parsed literals. A literal string is a string where what you type is exactly what you get.

```
$flavor = "mint chocolate chip";
println('I love $flavor $+ !!!');
```

I love $flavor $+ !!!

Enclose literal strings in single quotes. Pay special attention to which types of quotes you use as there is a difference between literal strings and parsed literal strings.

Parsed Literals

Parsed literal strings replace *$scalar* variables with their value.

```
$flavor = "mint chocolate chip";
println("I love $flavor $+ !!!");
```

```
I love mint chocolate chip!!!
```

Parsed literals only evaluate variables beginning with a $ sign. Surround variables with whitespace to allow the parsed literal to extract the variable name. The $+ value acts as a concatenation operator to remove unwanted whitespace within parsed literals.

```
$super = "Super";
$mang  = "man";

println("Oh no! Where is $super $+ $mang $+ ???");
```

```
Oh no! Where is Superman???
```

Wait, there's more. Parsed literals also support built-in formatting for scalars.

```
$first = "First";
$last  = "Last";
$worth = "Worth";

println("$[10]first $[10]last $[-6]worth");
println("-" x 28);

$first = "John";
$last  = "Doe";
$worth = "12K";

println("$[10]first $[10]last $[-6]worth");

$first = "John";
$last  = "Deer";
$worth = "-45K";

println("$[10]first $[10]last $[-6]worth");
```

```
First      Last       Worth
----------------------------
John       Doe          12K
John       Deer        -45K
```

The built-in formatting aligns values to a set number of spaces. Specify the number within square brackets. By default, Sleep pads the value with spaces to the right. If you specify a negative number, the interpreter pads with spaces to the left.

You may also use an expression within the square brackets.

Escape characters within a parsed literal with the back slash character. The interpreter ignores the character immediately following a back slash. The interpreter also removes the initial backslash during processing. Some escaped characters have special meanings.

Escape	Description
`\n`	newline character
`\r`	return character
`\t`	tab character
`\u####`	16 bit unicode character i.e. "\u0063" is "c"
`\x##`	8 bit character i.e. "\x6A" is "j"
`\\`	back slash \ character

Sleep provides these operations for use with Strings.

Operator	Description
.	concatenation
x	string multiplication (i.e. `"a" x 3 = "aaa"`)
cmp	string comparison

Sleep has numerous functions that parse and manipulate strings. `&left` and `&right` extract left most and right most characters. `&substr` and `&mid` extract substrings from a string. `&split` breaks a string up into tokens with a delimiter and `&join` puts it back together again. `&replaceAt` and `&strrep` substitute substrings for other strings. And `&strlen` is used to find out the length of a string.

```
$ java -jar sleep.jar
>> Welcome to the Sleep scripting language
> x strlen("this is a test")
14
> x split(" ", "this is a test")
@('this', 'is', 'a', 'test')
> x replaceAt("this is a test", "is not", 5, 2)
this is not a test
> x uc("this is a ...")
THIS IS A ...
```

Many string functions allow the use of negative indices when specifying a character position. Sleep adds a negative index to the string length to obtain the real offset.

```
> x substr("this is a test!!", -6, -2)
test
> x indexOf("this is a test!!", "s", -6)
12
> x charAt("this is a test!!", -4)
s
```

3. Data Structures

3.1 Arrays

Sleep scalars store one-piece of data. An int, a string, or perhaps an object. Sometimes it helps to combine multiple pieces of data into one place. To this end Sleep has two data structures: the cuddly array and loveable hash.

An array is a container that stores data in numerical order. You can recall a piece of data from an array based on the data's position in the array. I sometimes refer to this position as the index. Array positions always begin at 0. Array scalars have an at sign (such as `@foo`) as the first character in their name. This type information in the variable name allows Sleep to create an empty array if one doesn't exist.

```
$x = 3;
@foo[0] = "Raphael";
@foo[1] = 42.5;
@foo[2] = "Donatello";
@foo[$x] = "Michelangelo";
```

This example populates *@foo* with some values. Referring to *@foo* will refer to the entire array itself. The square brackets next to the variable name are the index operator. This operator accepts any Sleep expression and tries to recall a value from the data structure to the left of it. In this example I use `0`, `1`, `2`, and `$x` to indiciate positions of *@foo*. *@foo* has the following contents when this example is complete:

Value	Index
"Raphael"	0
42.5	1
"Donatello"	2
"Michelangelo"	3

The string representation of this same array is:

```
@('Raphael', 42.5, 'Donatello', 'Michelangelo')
```

When referencing an array with the index operator, it is acceptable to use negative indices. You can use `@foo[-1]` to reference the last item of *@foo*. Most array functions normalize negative indices. Sleep subtracts a negative index from the array size to get the real index.

```
@array = @("a", "b", "c", "d", "e");

# insert "foo" into second from last element.
add(@array, "foo", -2);
println(@array);

# print last element of @array
println(@array[-1]);
```

```
@('a', 'b', 'c', 'd', 'foo', 'e')
e
```

You can assign arrays to each other as well. As stated in chapter 2, assigning an array to another array just copies the reference. Both *@array*'s will point to the same data. A change in one array will affect the other array.

```
@a = @("a", "b", "c");
@b = @a;
@b[1] = "!!!";

# see what I mean.

println("@a: " . @a);
println("@b: " . @b);
```

```
@a: @('a', '!!!', 'c')
@b: @('a', '!!!', 'c')
```

The function `&size` takes an array as a parameter and returns the total number of items in the array.

```
@a = @("a", "b", "c", "d", "e");
$size = size(@a);

println($size);
```

```
5
```

Use the `&remove` function to remove an item from an array.

```
@array = @("a", "b", "c", "3", "blah", 3, 3.0);
remove(@array, 3, "b");

println(@array);
```

```
@('a', 'c', 'blah', 3.0)
```

Arrays returned by built-in functions may be read-only. Functions that try to modify a read-only array will fail with a hard error message. See the documentation for an individual function to find out if the return value is read-only or not.

```
@files = ls("/");
shift(@files);
```

```
Warning: array is read-only at shiftls.sl:2
```

When in doubt, use `©` to copy a read-only array into something less whiney.

Multidimensional Arrays

Arrays are scalars just like numbers, objects, and strings. Since an array is a scalar that holds other scalars, it stands that an array can also hold other arrays. A multidimensional array is an array of arrays.

```
@data = @(
          @("a", "b", "c"),
          @(1, 2, 3, 4),
          @('.', '!', '#', '*')
        );
```

@data is a multidimensional array.

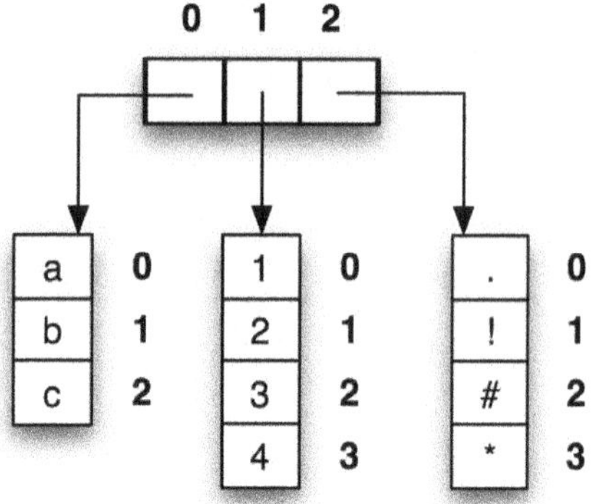

To access an item from *@data*:

```
$temp = @data[2][3]; # $temp is now '*'
```

This example stacks the index operator against another index operator. The index operator acts on the result of the expression to left of it. You can stack indices as deep as you like. Sleep knows from the variable name to create new empty arrays when you index into dimensions that don't yet exist.

Let us get back to the example. I could have setup the *@data* array with the following code:

```
@data[0][0] = "a";
@data[0][1] = "b";
@data[0][2] = "c";
@data[1][0] = 1;
@data[1][1] = 2;
@data[1][2] = 3;
@data[1][3] = 4;
@data[2][0] = '.';
@data[2][1] = '!';
@data[2][2] = '#';
@data[2][3] = '*';
```

Tuple Assignment

Tuple assignments allow you to assign items from an array to individual scalar values. A Sleep tuple is a comma separated list of variable names surrounded by parentheses on the left hand side of an assignment.

```
($x, $y, $z) = @array;
```

This example sets *$x* to the first item in *@array*, *$y* to the second item, and *$z* to the third item.

Tuple assignment sets the remaining scalars to *$null* when there are not enough items in *@array*.

Tuple assignment also works with individual values. If the value to assign is not an array, then all scalars in the tuple receive the same value. This form is useful for nulling out multiple values.

```
($a, $b, $c) = $null;
```

Assignment operations work with tuple assignment as well.

```
($x, $y, $z) += 3; # add 3 to $x, $y, and $z
```

You can also specify an array on the right hand side of a tuple assignment operation. This works as you would expect. Sleep applies the assignment operation to each scalar in the tuple and the corresponding array item.

```
($x, $y, $z) *= @(2, 3, 4); # $x = $x * 2; $y = $y * 3; etc..
```

Expand Array

Array expansion is a special case of tuple assignment operations. Wrap a single array scalar within a tuple to expand it. This is the same as typing `(@a[0], @a[1], ...)`. The rest of the tuple assignment rules apply. This has neat implications. For example to add two arrays:

```
@a = @(1, 2, 3);
@b = @(4, 5, 6);
(@a) += @b;

println("@a is: " . @a);
```

```
@a is: @(5, 7, 9)
```

Sorting Arrays

You can easily sort arrays with any criteria. The `&sort` function accepts a method for comparing two array items. Sleep also provides `&sorta` to sort arrays in alphabetical order. `&sortn` sorts integer or long arrays in numerical order and `&sortd` sorts double arrays.

```
sub caseInsensitiveCompare
{
   $a = lc($1);
   $b = lc($2);
```

```
    return $a cmp $b;
}

@array = @("zebra", "Xanadu", "ZooP", "ArDvArKS", "Arks", "bATS");
@sorted = sort(&caseInsensitiveCompare, @array);

println(@sorted);
```

```
@('ArDvArKS', 'Arks', 'bATS', 'Xanadu', 'zebra', 'ZooP')
```

Arrays: The Truth Revealed

There is something I must confess before we go further. Sleep arrays are not arrays. The Sleep array implementation uses a linked list. A linked list stores values in a chain. Each position knows only the previous and next position. To retrieve a value Sleep must walk through the list, value to value, until it locates the index. In small lists this is not likely to be noticed.

For large lists this can be a real performance bottleneck when not taken into account. Sorting and set operations are not efficient with lists. For these operations Sleep copies the list into the most suitable data structure, works on it, and then places the result into a list.

You may be thinking: "Wow, this is terrible. What possessed you to use linked lists?"

Many of Sleep's operations allow you to add or remove elemements to and from the beginning, end, and middle of an array. Linked lists are excellent for this. Linked lists also scale as large as you like without slowdown for many operations.

3.2 Stacks, Lists, and Sets

I just alluded to the idea that arrays are far more than containers that store their values with a numerical index. In this section I will introduce you to other capabilities of the mighty array.

Stacks

A stack is a first-in last-out data structure. My father pays his bills once a month. He hasn't heard of online bill paying yet. You can tell him. I tried. Anyways, when a bill arrives he places it on his desk on top of a stack of other bills. When payment time comes he reaches for the top bill and starts to work on it. The last bill he placed on the stack is the first one he works on.

You can use Sleep arrays as stacks. The last position in the array is the top of the stack. The first position is the bottom. Use &push to add data to the top position. Also &pop will remove and return the data from the top position.

```
push(@stack, "apple");
push(@stack, "banana");
push(@stack, "cucumber");

println("Stack is: " . @stack);

$value = pop(@stack);
println("Top item is: " . $value);

println("Stack is: " . @stack);
```

```
Stack is: @('apple', 'banana', 'cucumber')
Top item is: cucumber
Stack is: @('apple', 'banana')
```

Voila, with this example we have a stack of fruit.

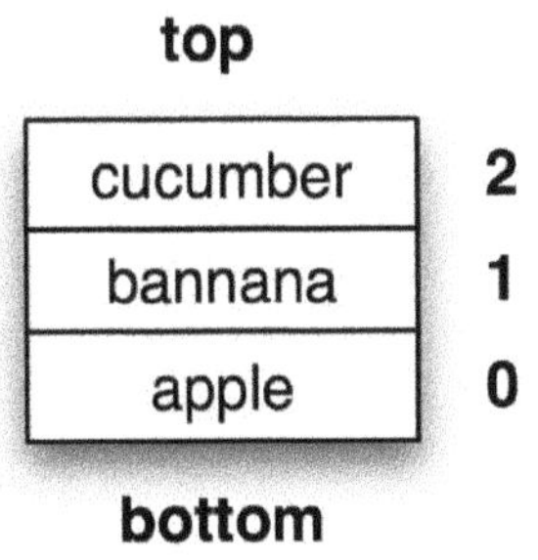

top	
cucumber	2
bannana	1
apple	0
bottom	

Queues

Similar to stacks are queues. Queues are first-in, first-out data structures. Use &shift to remove and return the first item of an array.

```
@queue = @("bottom", "middle", "top");
$bottom = shift(@queue);

println($bottom);
println("Queue is: " . @queue);
```

```
bottom
Queue is: @('middle', 'top')
```

Lists

I already discussed linked lists a few sections ago. It would be a crime to not provide some list operations in Sleep. It helps to think of a list as a head (first item) followed by everything else (all items beyond the first). Grab the head of a list by indexing position 0 of an array. Use `&sublist` to get everything else.

```
@list = @("a", "b", "c");

# car/head of list...
println(@list[0]);

# cdr/rest of list
println(sublist(@list, 1));
```

```
a
@('b', 'c')
```

The `&sublist` function returns a slice of a list. Changes to a sublist affect the parent list.

```
@array = @("a", "b", "c", @("dd", "ee", "ff"), "g", "h");
@sub = sublist(@array, 2, 4);

# note that an array scalar counts as 1 element.
println(@sub);

# modifications to the sublist also affect the parent.
@sub[1] = "what happened?";
println(@sub);
println(@array);
```

```
@('c', @('dd', 'ee', 'ff'))
@('c', 'what happened?')
@('a', 'b', 'c', 'what happened?', 'g', 'h')
```

@array prior to modifications:

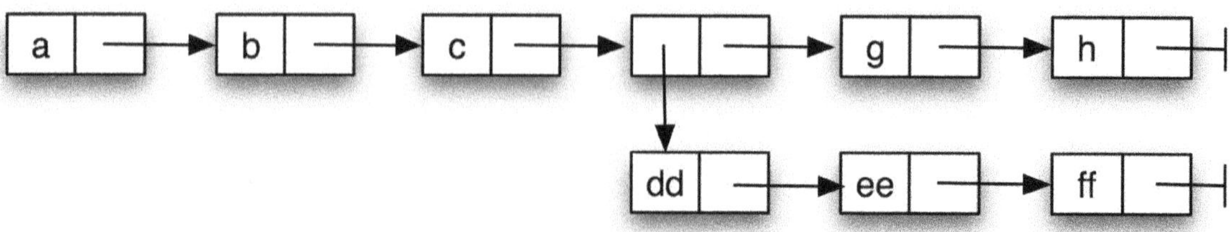

The sublist of *@array* consisting of positions 2-4 (up to but not including 4):

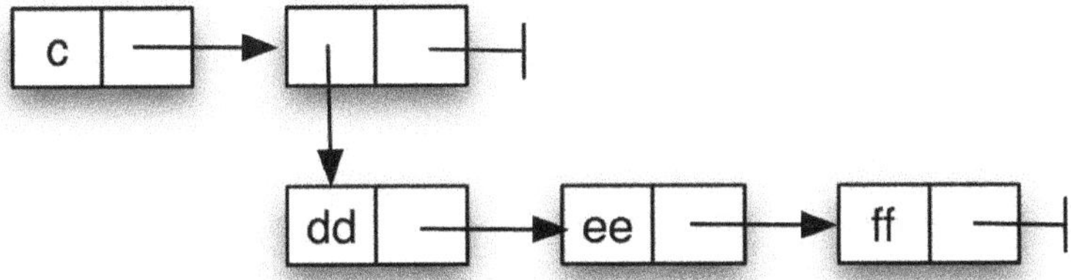

Sleep creates sublists in constant time. A sublist is nothing more than a view into the parent list.

Sets and Scalar Identity

A set is a collection of values. The order of these values doesn't matter. What matters in sets is membership: testing if a value is in a set or not. A naive algorithm for set membership would simply compare a value to every item in the set. If the value is equal to any of the set members then it is in the set.

Certain set operations are possible with arrays. Sleep uses **scalar identity** to decide if two scalars are equivalent. The identity algorithm compares references for object scalars and function scalars. The identity function uses the string representation to compare other scalars. You can explicitly compare scalar identity with the =~ predicate.

```
$ java -jar sleep.jar
>> Welcome to the Sleep scripting language
> ? 3 =~ "3"
true
> ? 3 =~ "4"
false
```

Test if a value is a member of an array with the `in` predicate.

```
> ? 3 in @("3", "4", "5", "a")
true
> ? "b" in @("3", "4", "5", "a")
false
```

The union operation places the values of two sets into one set. Values that were in either set are members of the resulting set. Sleep supports the union of two arrays with the `&addAll` function.

The difference operation removes all values present in one set from another. A value will be a member of only one of the resulting sets. Sleep does set difference with the `&removeAll` function.

Finally there is the intersect operation. The intersection of two sets is all the values the two sets have in common. `&retainAll` provides the intersection operation.

```
@setA = @("apple", "ardvarks", "apes");
@setB = @("bats", "baseballs", "books", "apes");

# union operation:

@result = addAll(copy(@setA), @setB);
println("A union B: " . @result);

# difference operation:

@result = removeAll(copy(@setA), @setB);
println("A difference B: " . @result);

# intersect operation:

@result = retainAll(copy(@setA), @setB);
println("A intersect B: " . @result);
```

```
A union B: @('apple', 'ardvarks', 'apes', 'bats', 'baseballs', 'books')
A difference B: @('apple', 'ardvarks')
A intersect B: @('apes')
```

The results of these set operations on *@setA* and *@setB* are shown in this Venn diagram:

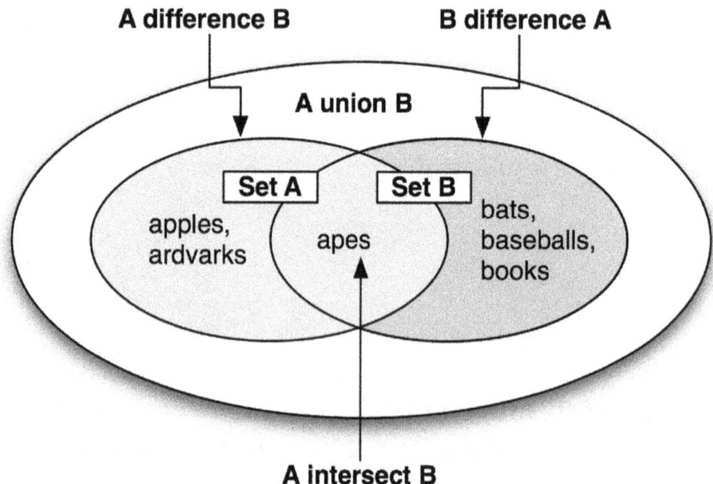

3.3 Hashes

Hash scalars hold multiple values associated with a key. Use the percent symbol at the beginning of hash names. Sleep uses this type information to create an empty hash when needed.

```
$x = 3;
%foo["name"] = "Raphael";
%foo["job"]  = "wasting time";
%foo[$x]     = "Michelangelo";

println("%foo is: " . %foo);
```

```
%foo is: %(3 => 'Michelangelo', job => 'wasting time', name => 'Raphael')
```

You can specify hashes in place. The syntax is a percent sign followed by parentheses enclosing a comma separated list of key value pairs. Specify a key value pair with the => operator.

```
%hash = %(a => "apple", b => "boy", c => 3 * (9 % 7));

println("%hash is: " . %hash);
```

```
%hash is: %(a => 'apple', c => 6, b => 'boy')
```

Hash keys are always converted to strings. For example `3` refers to the same value as `"3"`. Use the index operator to retrieve values from a hash.

```
%hash = %(a => 'apple', b => 'boy');
%hash["c"] = "cow";

println("%hash is:        " . %hash);
println("%hash['c'] is: " . %hash["c"]);
```

```
%hash is:      %(a => 'apple', c => 'cow', b => 'boy')
%hash['c'] is: cow
```

You can also assign hashes to eachother. This is the same as assigning an array to another array. Assigning a hash to another hash copies the reference. Both hash variables refer to the same data.

Some built-in functions return read-only hashes. Functions that try to modify a read-only hash will fail with a hard error message. Use `©` to create a copy of a read-only hash.

To remove a key from a hash set the item to *$null* or use `&removeAt`. To remove a value use the `&remove` function.

Use &keys to get an array of keys in a hash. Hash keys are unordered.

```
%data = %(a => "AT-ST Walker", b => "bat", c => "cat", d => 43);

foreach $var (keys(%data))
{
   println($var);
}
```

```
d
a
c
b
```

Ordered Hashes

Actually, I lied. Not all hashes have unordered keys. These are ordered hashes. Ordered hashes created with &ohash keep track of insertion order. The oldest key is at the beginning of the list and the newest key is at the end. The &ohasha keeps track of access order. The access ordered hash moves keys to the end of the order after each request. With access ordered hashes the first key is the least recently used key.

```
%random = %(a => "apple", b => "boy", c => "cat", d => "dog");
println("Random:  " . %random);

%ordered = ohash(a => "apple", b => "boy", c => "cat", d => "dog");
println("Ordered: " . %ordered);
```

```
Random:  %(d => 'dog', a => 'apple', c => 'cat', b => 'boy')
Ordered: %(a => 'apple', b => 'boy', c => 'cat', d => 'dog')
```

Ordered hashes may have hit and removal policies associated with them. Sleep calls the removal policy prior to adding a new key. The removal policy decides wether to remove the key at the beginning of the list or not. Sleep invokes the miss policy when a key with no value is requested.

```
%answers = ohash();

setMissPolicy(%answers,
{
   return 42; # default value
});

println(%answers);

println(%answers["life"]);
println(%answers["the universe"]);
```

```
println(%answers["everything"]);

println(%answers);
```

```
%()
42
42
42
%(life => 42, the universe => 42, everything => 42)
```

The removal policy coupled with the access ordered hash makes a great least recently used cache mechanism. We will explore this further in chapter 8.

Mixing Arrays/Hashes

Multidimensional hashes work the same as Sleep arrays. A hash is a scalar that holds other scalar. Hashes can hold arrays, scalars, and other hashes. Arrays can hold hashes as well.

```
%hash = %(letters => @("a", "b", "c", "d"),
                names   => %(
                                rsm => "Raphael Mudge",
                                fvm => "Frances Mudge")
            );
```

Sleep will create a new hash or array when a script tries to index to a nonexistent level. Sleep uses the variable name at the start of the index stack to decide which data structure to create.

The index operator is merely an operator. It operates on values, not variable names. You can apply the index operator to function calls, expressions, and *$scalars*. Sleep will return *$null* after trying to index a new level in these contexts.

```
$temp = split(' ', "A B C")[1]; # $temp is now "B"
```

Circular References

Sleep makes some concessions to allow arrays and hashes to reference themselves. These are circular references. You can use this feature to represent graphs in Sleep.

Nodes and edges make a graph. Edges connect one node to another.

The array and hash string description points out a circular dependency with a `@` or `%` followed by a number. Count the number of opening parentheses from the left to find the data structure the number refers to.

```
# node $n: $n[0] = arbitrary data; $n[1 .. n] = edges

sub node
{
   return @($1);
}

sub add_edge
{
   push($1, $2);
}

$a = node("a");
$b = node("b");
$c = node("c");

add_edge($a, $b);

add_edge($b, $a);
add_edge($b, $c);
add_edge($b, $b);

add_edge($c, $c);

println("a: $a");
println("b: $b");
println("c: $c");
```

```
a: @('a', @('b', @0, @('c', @2), @1))
b: @('b', @('a', @0), @('c', @2), @0)
c: @('c', @0)
```

This graph is shown here.

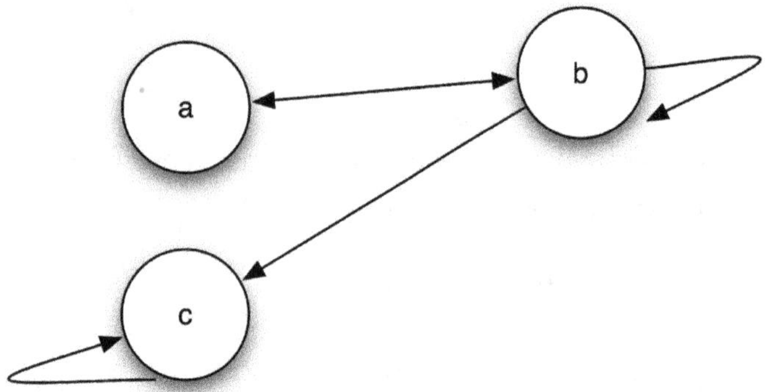

Each node is an array. The first item of the array is the value of the node. The rest of the array items represent the outgoing edges from the node.

4. Flow Control

4.1 Comparisons

Flow control is the art of adding logic to your script. The constructs presented here will allow your programs to make decisions based on conditions. There are even constructs for iterating through the various Sleep data structures. I will start with the if-statement.

If/else statements let you compare different values and execute a certain part of the script based on the result of the comparison.

```
if (v1 operator v2)
{
   # .. code to execute ..
}
else if (-operator v3)
{
   # .. more code to execute ..
}
else
{
   # do this if nothing above it is true
}
```

An if-statement checks a predicate expression. Sleep executes the next block of code if the expression is true. Sleep supports binary and unary predicate expressions. A predicate expression asks a question about data. For example the eq predicate asks: "Are these two strings equal?" After the if-statement any number of optional if-else blocks may follow.

Sleep checks these in order. The interpreter stops checking once one of the if-statements in the chain succeeds. Sleep defaults to the else block after all other if-statements fail.

These predicate operators compare numbers.

Operator	Description
==	equal to
!=	not equal to
<	less than
>	greater than
<=	less than or equal to
>=	greater than or equal to

These predicate operators compare strings.

Operator	Description
eq	equal to
ne	not equal to
lt	less than
gt	greater than
isin	is substring v1 contained in string v2
`iswm`	is string v1 a wildcard match of string v2

Why does sleep have separate comparisons for strings and numbers?

Sleep tries to fit values to the context of an operator. For example, the numerical comparison == expects two numbers. This operator will cast anything it sees into a number. The `eq` comparison expects two strings. As a scripter, you need to be aware of what comparison is taking place. For example the string "3" and the double 3.0 are equivalent with ==. When you compare these values as strings, `"3"` and `"3.0"` are not the same string. For these reasons Sleep has separate comparisons for strings and numbers.

This last set of predicates compares scalars by identity and reference.

Operator	Description
=~	is v1 equal to v2 under the rules of scalar identity (3.2 Fun with Arrays)
`is`	compare the object reference v1 to the object reference v2

Example: Guessing Game

This example showcases all the skills up to this point in the chapter. It is the ever-classic guessing game. Simply tell the computer what number it is thinking of to win.

```
# most people think of the number 4 or 7 when asked
# to think of something 1-10... this program will to.

$number = rand(@(4, 7));

# read in a number

print("What number am I thinking of? ");
$guess = readln();

# check the guess.

if ($guess == $number)
{
   println("You got it!! You must be psychic");
}
else if ($guess < $number)
{
   println("Too low... you lose!");
}
else if ($guess > $number)
{
   println("Too high, you still lose");
}

println("The number was $number $+ , thanks for playing");
```

$ **java -jar sleep.jar guess.sl**
What number am I thinking of? **2**
Too low... you lose!
The number was 7, thanks for playing

$ **java -jar sleep.jar guess.sl**
What number am I thinking of? **4**
You got it!! You must be psychic
The number was 4, thanks for playing

This example uses an if, else-if, else-if chain. This program gets the guess with `&readln`. The `&readln` function returns a string. This is a nonissue as the number comparisons convert the string to an integer.

Combining Comparisons

Combine comparisons with the logic operators && (AND) and || (OR). These operators evaluate each predicate condition in order.

```
sub check
{
   if (($1 > 0) && ($1 <= 10))
   {
      println("$1 is within 0 .. 10");
   }
   else
   {
      println("$1 is out of range!!");
   }
}

check(5);
check(88888888);
```

5 is within 0 .. 10
88888888 is out of range!!

This example defines a subroutine to check if a value is within the range of 1 to 10.

Sleep short circuits comparisons. With AND, if `$1 > 0` is false, then Sleep never evaluates the next statement `$1 <= 10` as the whole comparison is already false. With OR, if one of the arguments is true, then the whole expression is already true and evaluation stops.

To avoid confusing the Sleep parser it "helps" to put parentheses around the predicate expressions. For example: `(a comparison) && (another comparison) && (who cares)`. The parser does not always need these parentheses but they may make your code cleaner.

You can use as many && and || to create logical chains of comparisons as complex as you like. The comparison `($x == 3) || (($x < 0) && ($x > 10))` evaluates to true for any *$x* value equivalent to three or less than zero and greater than ten.

Negation

You can negate most comparisons by inserting an exclamation point before the predicate operator.

```
if ("I" !isin "Team")
{
   println("There is no 'I' in Team");
```

```
}

if ("m" isin "Team" && "e" isin "Team")
{
   println("... but there is an m and an e");
}
```

There is no 'I' in Team
... but there is an m and an e

This example checks the string `"Team"` does not contain the substring `"I"`. Of course I can't mention there is no `"I"` in `"Team"` without elluding to the fact the letters to form the word `"me"` are present.

Unary Predicates

Until now all the predicates have been binary predicates. Sleep supports unary (one argument) predicates as well. Unary predicates always begin with a dash character.

Operator	Description
-isarray	is v1 a scalar array
-isfunction	does v1 reference a function
-ishash	is v1 a scalar hash
-isletter	is v1 a letter
-isnumber	is v1 a number
-istrue	is v1 "true"

Negate a unary predicate by prefixing the dash with an exclamantion point:

$ **java -jar sleep.jar**
>> Welcome to the Sleep scripting language
> **? -isnumber 3**
true
> **? !-isnumber 3**
false
> **? !-isnumber "Zebras"**
true

What is truth

Truth is all relative. Here, true means any value that is not the empty string, not zero, and not *$null*. Everything else is true.

Why does truth matter? Some comparisons do not contain a predicate expression. Sometimes you can use a scalar value by itself as the comparison for an if statement. A scalar that meets the true value rules will evaluate to true.

```
sub check
{
   if ($1)
   {
      println("' $+ $1 $+ ' is true!");
   }
   else
   {
      println("' $+ $1 $+ ' is false :(");
   }
}

check("the truth!");
check(0);
check("");
check("0");
```

```
'the truth!' is true!
'0' is false :(
'' is false :(
'0' is false :(
```

The Conditional Operator

Sleep supports the conditional operator `iff`. The first parameter to `iff` is a predicate expression. The conditional operator short circuits arguments. Sleep evaluates and returns the second argument when the predicate expression is true. Sleep will evaluate and return the third argument when the predicate expression is false. If you neglect to provide a second or third argument the `iff` function will use 1 and `$null`.

```
sub showTime
{
   $time = int((ticks() - $time) / 1000);
   println($time . " second" . iff($time != 1, "s"));
}

$time = ticks();

# do some sort of intensive operation here...
sleep(3600);

showTime();
```

3 seconds

The conditional operator simplifies the output for this example.

Debugging Comparisons

Sometimes when programming it helps to know what decisions your program is making, with what information, and to what outcome. Many times programmers do a poor man's debug by using `&println` statements all over the place to figure out what is happening. Sleep's built-in `&debug` function includes a mode to trace all logical comparisons. This mode can help you track down potential logic issues. Set this flag with `debug(debug() | 64)`.

```
debug(debug() | 64); # enable DEBUG_TRACE_LOGIC

$favorite = "chocolate";

if ($favorite == "mint chocolate")
{
   println("I like mint chocolate chip!");
}
```

Trace: 'chocolate' == 'mint chocolate' ? TRUE at tracelogic.sl:5
I like mint chocolate chip!

From the example above you may notice a counterintuitive result. The logic traceing shows that two separate strings are equal to eachother with the == predicate. This should offer an indiciation that something is wrong (using == instead of `eq` for strings is a common mistake). With this functionality you will know to look at the == operator more closely to figure out what is happening. You may recall that == is for numbers. Both strings converted to numbers evaluate to `0`.

4.2 Loops

Loops are a mechanism for counting bottles of beer programatically. A loop executes while a condition holds true. Sleep has four looping constructs. I cover each of these constructs in this section.

While Loops

A while loop executes a series of statements while a comparison evaluates to true.

The syntax for a while loop is:

```
while (comparison) { code }
```

Now I'd like to demonstrate "99 Bottles of Beer?" with a while loop.

```
# 99 Bottles of Beer on the Wall
# while loop version.

$total = 99;
while ($total > 0)
{
   $beer  = "$total bottle" . iff($total == 1, "", "s");

   println("$beer of beer on the wall, $beer of beer.");
   $total = $total - 1;

   if ($total == 0)
   {
      println("Take one down and pass it around, no more bottles of beer 
on the wall");
   }
   else
   {
      $beer  = "$total bottle" . iff($total == 1, "", "s");
      println("Take one down and pass it around, $beer of beer on the 
wall.");
   }
   println();
}

println("No more bottles of beer on the wall, no more bottles of beer.");
println("Go to the store and buy some more, 99 bottles of beer on the 
wall.");
```

While loops provide the most flexibility over how the loop works.

For Loops

For loops are similar. The for loop consolidates the initialization, comparison, and increment statements into one statement.

```
for (initialization; comparison; increment) { code }
```

For loops allow empty statements in the intialization and increment fields. These fields also allow multiple statements. Separate statements with a comma.

The `break` and `continue` commands affect the body of the for loop. The increment step still executes. This is one of the key differences between a for loop and a while loop.

More beer?

```
for ($total = 99; $total > 0; $total--, $beer = "$total bottle")
{
   $beer = $beer . iff($total == 1, "", "s");
   println("$beer of beer on the wall, $beer of beer.");

   if (($total - 1) == 0)
   {
      println("Take one down and pass it around, no more bottles of beer
on the wall.");
   }
   else
   {
      $beer = ($total - 1) . " bottle" . iff($total == 1, "", "s");
      println("Take one down and pass it around, $beer of beer on the
wall.");
   }
   println();
}

println("No more bottles of beer on the wall, no more bottles of beer.");
println("Go to the store and buy some more, 99 bottles of beer on the
wall.");
```

Use for loops when you can isolate your **initialization** and **increment** statements from the **code**.

Assignment Loops

An assignment loop executes a block of code while an expression evaluates to a non-*$null* value. The assignment loop evaluates **expression** and assigns to the **variable** each iteration.

```
while variable (expression) { code }
```

Assignment loops are great at reading files line by line.

```
$handle = openf("readfile.sl");

while $read (readln($handle))
{
   # do something useful.
}
```

Use assignment loops when you want to evaluate an expression and operate on its value until it is *$null*.

Foreach Loops

Similar to the assignment loop is the foreach loop. Foreach loops take either a function, an array, or a hash scalar and iterate over each item.

Foreach loops note the index and value of each iteration. For arrays and functions the index is a counter that starts at zero. The hash scalar uses the dictionary key as the index. In this form the value is the data at the current index.

```
foreach index => value (source) { code }
```

Optionally the foreach loop can assign just the value of each iteration. In the case of a hash, this form will provide the dictionary key.

```
foreach value (source) { code }
```

Changes to the **value** will change the value in the source.

```
%data = %(foo => "a", bar => "b", baz => "c", jaz => "d");

foreach $key => $value (%data)
{
   if ($value eq "c")
   {
      $value = "coolios";
   }
}

println(%data);
```

```
%(foo => 'a', baz => 'coolios', bar => 'b', jaz => 'd')
```

Avoid functions that change the structure of the source during foreach loops. This means `&push`, `&pop`, and friends against the source are off-limits during a foreach loop.

You may remove the current value during a foreach loop. Use the `&remove` function with no arguments.

```
@data = @(8, 7, 6, 5, 4, 3, 2, 1, 0);

foreach $index => $value (@data)
{
   if ($index == $value)
   {
      println("$index == $value !!!");
      remove();
   }
```

```
}

println(@data);
```

```
4 == 4 !!!
@(8, 7, 6, 5, 3, 2, 1, 0)
```

The foreach loop calls a function each iteration to iterate over it. The foreach loop terminates when the function returns *$null*.

```
sub range
{
   # Returns a new function that returns the next number in the
   # range with each call.  Returns $null at the end of the range

   # Don't worry, closures will come in the next chapter :)
   return lambda(
   {
      return iff($begin <= $end, $begin++ - 1, $null);
   }, $begin => $1, $end => $2);
}

foreach $value (range(8, 13))
{
   println($value);
}
```

```
8
9
10
11
12
13
```

Foreach loops are useful for iterating over a data structure. The foreach loop is ideal for iterating over arrays. Each iteration walks one element of the linked list providing the best performance.

Loop Control

Use `break` and `continue` to alter the flow of control within a loop.

The `break` command immediately terminates the current loop.

```
for ($x = 0; $x < 10; $x++)
{
   if ($x == 3)
   {
```

```
        break;
    }
    println($x);
}
println("done!");
```

0
1
2
done!

The `continue` command causes an immediate jump to the next iteration of the current loop.

```
for ($x = 0; $x < 10; $x++)
{
    if ($x > 2 && $x < 8)
    {
        continue;
    }
    println($x);
}
println("done!");
```

0
1
2
8
9
done!

4.3 Exceptions

Sleep supports the exception paradigm for error management. Sometimes an error occurs that you don't want to handle in your code. This error is an exceptional condition. You can send this condition through all calling functions with the `throw` command.

Use the `throw` command to stop the current function and send the condition up to the first exception handler. Sleep ignores the `throw` command when the thrown value is *$null*.

```
sub multiplyBy3
{
    if (!-isnumber $1)
    {
        throw "&multipyBy3( $+ $1 $+ ) requires a number!";
    }
```

```
    return $1 * 3;
}
```

This subroutine checks if an argument is a number. If your program calls `multiplyBy3("hi")` then the exception `"&mulityBy3(hi) requires a number!"` is sent up the call stack. Sleep searches the calling functions for an exception handler. When one is found the handler executes. An exception allows scripts to jump out of the current execution context to deal with an error. An uncaught exception will cause the script to exit.

Sleep exceptions don't bubble up to the Java runtime environment. The only exception to this is when an exception is thrown within a proxy instance. 7.2 Parameter Marshalling: Proxy Instances covers them in detail.

Now we will look at how to install a handler and catch exceptions.

```
try
{
    multiplyBy3("hi");
}
catch $message
{
    warn("Failed to multiply by 3: $message");
    printAll(getStackTrace());
}
```

```
Warning: Failed to multiply by 3: &multipyBy3(hi) requires a number! at eval:6
   eval:2 &multiplyBy3()
   eval:4 <origin of exception>
```

This example installs an exception handler with the try-catch block. The try block executes code that may result in an exception. Sleep calls the catch block when any exception occurs. Exceptions bubble up. So if you call a function that calls a function that throws an exception and no other try-catch block is in place, your catch block will receive the exception.

The catch block assigns the exception to the variable specified with the catch keyword. In this example the exception is available as *$message*.

The function `&getStackTrace` returns the call stack at the time of the exception. Use this to deduce your programs behavior.

Use the `&warn` function to communicate an error message to Sleep. This function is more generic than `&println`. It will work regardless of where Sleep is embedded. `&warn` also outputs the current script name and line number.

Choice in Error Handling

Sleep does not use exceptions as the default error mechanism. Soft errors are available with the `&checkError` function. A soft error is a non-fatal error. An error resulting from the failure to open a file is a soft error. The `&checkError` function returns and clears the most recent error. As a side note `debug(debug() | 2)` will print a notification when an error is available to `&checkError`.

```
$handle = openf("doesNotExist");

if (checkError($error))
{
   warn("error: $error");
   return;
}

println("file opened!");
```

> Warning: error: java.io.FileNotFoundException: /Users/raffi/manual/manual/doesNotExist (No such file or directory) at choice0.sl:5

You can throw individual errors yourself. Insert `throw checkError($error);` in your script to throw an error if there is one. `&checkError` will return *$null* when there is no error. You may recall that `throw` will not act on *$null* values.

```
try
{
   $handle = openf("doesNotExist");
   throw checkError($error);

   println("file opened!");
}
catch $exception
{
   warn("error: $exception");
}
```

> Warning: error: java.io.FileNotFoundException: /Users/raffi/manual/manual/doesNotExist (No such file or directory) at choice1.sl:10

Sleep supports a debug option to throw all errors. You can enable this option with `debug(debug() | 34)`. This debug option will immediately throw an exception as soon as an error is made available.

```
debug(34);

try
```

```
{
   $handle = openf("doesNotExist");
   # la la la... do stuff...

   println("file opened!");
}
catch $exception
{
   warn("error: $exception");
}
```

Warning: error: java.io.FileNotFoundException: /Users/raffi/manual/manual/doesNotExist (No such file or directory) at choice2.sl:12

The `&checkError` mechanism for handling errors is simple. It requires little code on your part. It also supports automatic reporting through debug level 2. The try-catch mechanism requires more code. However the try-catch mechanism gives you a stack trace and allows you to deal with errors and recovery in one place. When writing applications in Sleep I use the try-catch mechanism. With this mechanism I feel comfortable that my program will better recover from unforeseen circumstances. When writing quick hacks (which I am known to do), I simply enable debug level 2. Ultimately the choice is yours.

4.4 Assertions

Assertions are a simple script debug mechanism. An assertion statement is a guard that makes sure a condition is true. Sleep will exit with an error message if the condition isn't true. The syntax for an assertion is:

```
assert condition;
```

You can attach a message to an assertion. This message is shown when the condition fails:

```
assert condition : message;
```

Assertions are great for last minute sanity checks. Can you tell what is wrong with this code snippet?

```
sub fact
{
   return iff($1 == 0, 1, $1 * fact($1 - 1));
}
```

The factorial function expects a positive number. A negative number would cause this script to go into an infinite loop. Assertions enforce these expectations (sometimes called preconditions).

```
sub fact
{
   assert $1 >= 0 : "invalid arg for fact: $1";
   return iff($1 == 0, 1, $1 * fact($1 - 1));
}

println(fact(-10));
```

Warning: invalid arg for fact: -10 at badfact2.sl:3

One reason programmers shy away from extra guards is performance fears. Sleep enables the assertions feature by default. Set the `sleep.assert` property to false to disable assertions. Chapter 1 discusses how to do this. The parser ignores all assert statements when assertions are off.

```
# this program will quit early when
# assertions are enabled

assert 2 + 2 : "eh, assertions are enabled";
println("Whee...");
```

$ **java -jar sleep.jar compare.sl**
Warning: eh, assertions are enabled at compare.sl:4
$ **java -Dsleep.assert=false -jar sleep.jar compare.sl**
Whee...

Take care that your assertion statements are free of side effect. A side effect is some change to the current state of the script. Assertions with side effects are a potential source of subtle bugs when disabled.

5. Functions

5.1 Subroutines

Sleep subroutines are mini programs. You can call them, with arguments, and they give back a value.

```
sub add
{
   return $1 + $2;
}

$x = add(3, 4);
```

This example is an add subroutine. *$x* receives the result from the add subroutine. In this example the result is seven. Separate arguments with a comma. In this example `3` and `4` are arguments.

Within a function arguments are available by their number. I refer to these as anonymous arguments. `$1` is the first argument, `$2` the second, and `$3` the third.

The array `@_` also contains all of the anonymous arguments for a subroutine.

The return command stops the subroutine and gives a value back to the caller. The caller is the program that ran the subroutine.

Beware Side Effects: How arguments are passed

Sleep passes all subroutine arguments by reference. This is important to note. A change to an argument will affect the parent.

```
sub test
{
   $1 = "bar";
}

$fluffy = "foo";
test($fluffy);

println("The value of \$fluffy is $fluffy");
```

```
The value of $fluffy is bar
```

This feature makes it easy to shoot yourself in the foot. To avoid this behavior stay away from directly modifying arguments. A change to an argument is a side effect. Functions with side effects are a potential source of subtle bugs. You can use the `&watch` function to watch for scalar changes, just in case.

```
sub test
{
   $1 = "bar";
}

$fluffy = "foo";
watch('$fluffy');

test($fluffy);

println("The value of \$fluffy is $fluffy");
```

```
Warning: watch(): $fluffy = 'bar' at fluffy2.sl:3
The value of $fluffy is bar
```

Named Arguments

Use the key-value operator to pass a named argument. The key portion of the key-value operator is the variable name for the argument. Sleep places this value into the local scope of the function.

```
sub team
{
   println("$first is a member of team: $team");
}
```

```
team($first => "James", $team => "ramrod");
team($first => "Naji", $team => "ramrod");
team($first => "Jerard", $team => "ramnot");
```

James is a member of team: ramrod
Naji is a member of team: ramrod
Jerard is a member of team: ramnot

Named arguments do not affect the anonymous argument sequence or @_.

Arrays and Hashes as arguments

You can pass arrays and hashes as arguments to a function.

```
sub foo
{
   println("Third element is: " . $1[2]);
}

@array = @("a", "b", "c");
foo(@array);
```

Third element is: c

Recursion

Sleep supports recursion. A function that calls itself is recursive. Factorial is a common example:

```
sub fact
{
   if ($1 == 0)
   {
      return 1;
   }

   return $1 * fact($1 - 1);
}

$value = fact(11);
println("11! is $value");
```

11! is 39916800

Trace function calls

Sleep's trace mode allows you to trace function calls. This mode is set with the `&debug` function. This mode prints each function name, argument, and return value with the script name and line number. This tool is valuable for understanding your scripts. Debug trace is level 8.

```
debug(debug() | 8);

sub fact
{
   if ($1 == 1)
   {
      return 1;
   }

   return $1 * fact($1 - 1);
}

println("Result is: " . fact(5));
```

```
Trace: &fact(1) = 1 at trace.sl:10
Trace: &fact(2) = 2 at trace.sl:10
Trace: &fact(3) = 6 at trace.sl:10
Trace: &fact(4) = 24 at trace.sl:10
Trace: &fact(5) = 120 at trace.sl:13
Result is: 120
Trace: &println('Result is: 120') at trace.sl:13
```

Profile your scripts

Sleep sports a built-in profiler. The profile mode records function calls and the execution time. Debug trace collects profile statistics automatically. Use `&debug` level 24 to enable only the profiler. The `&profile` function provides the profiler statistics

```
debug(debug() | 24);

sub appendConcatOperator
{
   $string = "";
   for ($x = 0; $x < 8000; $x++)
   {
      $string = $string . "x";
   }
}

sub appendBuffer
```

```
{
   $string = "";
   $handle = allocate();
   for ($x = 0; $x < 8000; $x++)
   {
      writeb($handle, "x");
   }
   closef($handle);
   $string = readb($handle, available($handle));
}

# benchmark these 2 methods for building strings
appendBuffer();
appendConcatOperator();

# print out the profiler output
printAll(profile());
```

```
4.479s 1 &appendConcatOperator
0.372s 1 &appendBuffer
0.041s 8000 &writeb
0.0040s 1 &readb
0.0030s 1 &allocate
0.0010s 1 &closef
0.0s 1 &available
```

This example shows the profiler in action. Here I use two techniques for building a large string of data. One method uses the string concatenation operator within a for loop. The other uses a memory buffer and Sleep's I/O to build the string. The memory buffer is faster by an order of magnitude.

I will now give a very standard warning in the world of programming: Write code that works first. Once you have code that works use a profiler to find out where your code spends time. Optimize the slow portion if you must. Rinse, lather, and repeat until you have the performance you desire.

5.2 Scalar Scope

Sleep has three levels of variable scope. In this section I discuss global scope and local scope. I discuss the third, closure scope, later in this chapter. Scope defines where a scalar exists and how long it lasts for. A global scalar is accessible anywhere in a script. Global scalars exist for the lifetime of the program.

A local scalar is accessible during a function call. The variable exists while the function runs. Once the function exits the variable goes away. Local variables have higher precedence than global variables.

Use `&local` and `&global` to declare variables. These functions accept a string of variable names separated by whitespace. Sleep scalars have a global scope by default.

```
sub verdict
{
   local('$decision');
   $decision = "not guilty";
}

$decision = "guilty";
verdict();

# what is the value of $decision?
```

This example declares the subroutine verdict. The subroutine assigns a value to *$decision*. Which scalar gets the value? The local or global *$verdict*? Sleep assigns the value to the local scalar. This function does not affect the global scalar. When `&verdict` returns the local scalar goes away. So what is the final value of *$decision*? The answer is `"guilty"`.

Pass by Name

I introduced named arguments earlier in this chapter. A common use of named arguments is to pass a scalar into another script scope. Functions such as `&lambda`, `&fork`, and `&invoke` pass variables between scopes. Named arguments also pass variable between scopes. A function that has a local scalar *$x* can pass the local *$x* to another function with *foo($x => $x)*. Typing `$x => $x` gets tedious. It is also ugly to look at. And no one likes it. And it doesn't have any friends. And.. I spit on it!!! Ok. I'm beating a dead horse. Let me get a bigger club.

It is for this common case that pass by name exists. Prefix a variable with a backslash to pass it by name. For example: `foo(\$x)`. The parser compiles this form to `$x => $x` directly.

```
sub foo
{
   local('$explorer $year $password');
   $explorer = "Christopher Columbus";
   $year     = 1492;
   $password = "OceanBlue"; # not passed!

   bar(\$explorer, \$year);
}

sub bar
{
   println("The explorer is: $explorer");
```

```
   println("bumped around  : $year");
   println("password is    : $password");
}

foo();
```

```
The explorer is: Christopher Columbus
bumped around  : 1492
password is    :
```

You can use pass by name anywhere you would use the key-value operator.

Strict Mode

Sleep has a debug mode that requires scripts to declare all variables. This is strict mode. Set it with the `&debug` flag 4. Any attempt to use an undeclared variable in strict mode will fire a runtime warning. This warning will state the variable name, script name, and line number of the offending value.

Strict mode will help find bugs from the following errors:

- misspelled variable names
- bad assumptions about variable scope
- function calls with missing arguments

Declared variables are your friend. Here we find a misspelled variable name.

```
debug(debug() | 4);

sub foo
{
   local('$x');
   $xx = 3;
   return $x;
}

# why is this value null?
println("foo is: " . foo());
```

```
Warning: variable '$xx' not declared at declare.sl:6
foo is:
```

This example finds a scope mistake.

```
debug(debug() | 4);

sub foo
```

```
{
    local('$x');
    $x = 4;
    return bar();
}

sub bar
{
    $x = $x * 3;
    return $x;
}

# why does this output 0 and not 12?
println(foo());
```

```
Warning: variable '$x' not declared at declare2.sl:12
0
```

I highly recommend strict mode at all times.

Inline Subroutines

Sleep's solution to the macro is the inline subroutine. An inline subroutine executes within the current context. Inline subroutines inherit the local and closure variables of the calling function. Attempts to `yield`, `return`, or `callcc` will affect the parent.

Parameter passing to inline subroutines is the same as for normal subroutines. *$this* refers to the parent function and not the inline subroutine. Sleep restores the parent function's anonymous arguments upon returning from an inline subroutine.

Declares inline subroutines with the inline keyword.

```
inline printx
{
    println("\$x is $x");
}

sub foo
{
    local('$x');
    $x = 12345;
    printx();
}

foo();
```

```
$x is 12345
```

You can use &pushl to create a new local scope within an inline function. You can then declare variables within the local scope without worry. You must dispose of the local scope with &popl prior to the completion of the inline subroutine.

```
inline swap
{
   pushl($a => $1, $b => $2);

   local('$temp');
   $temp = $b;
   $b = $a;
   $a = $temp;

   popl();
}

sub bar
{
   local('$x $y $temp');
   $temp = 100;
   $x = 3;
   $y = 9;
   println("\$x: $x and \$y: $y");
   swap($x, $y);
   println("\$x: $x and \$y: $y (and $temp $+ )");
}

bar();
```

```
$x: 3 and $y: 9
$x: 9 and $y: 3 (and 100)
```

Do not call inline subroutines within an expression. The inline subroutine will return *$null.*

Inline subroutines can call other inline subroutines.

5.3 Closures

Sleep functions are first class types. You can assign them to variables, pass them as parameters to functions, and invoke them from a variable. A function scalar is an object scalar that references a `sleep.bridges.SleepClosure` object.

Subroutines declared with `sub` are named closures. You can refer to a named closure by prefixing an ampersand to its name. You can call closures with an object expression.

```
sub my_sub
{
   println("My name is: $1");
}

# same as my_sub("Raphael");
[&my_sub: "Raphael"];
```

My name is: Raphael

For named closures there isn't much excitement surrounding a new syntax. However this section focuses a lot on anonymous closures. Specify an anonymous closure with a block of code in place.

To assign an anonymous closure to a variable:

```
$closure = {
   println("My name is: $1");
};

[$closure: "Raphael"];
```

My name is: Raphael

You can also invoke an anonymous closure in an object expression. The object expression evaluates the object and assumes the result is a function it can call.

```
[{ println("Hello $1 $+ !"); } : "World!"];
```

Hello World!!

Use the `&setf` function to bind an anonymous closure to a name.

```
sub foo {
   println("foo!");
}

setf('&foo', { println("bar!"); });
foo();
```

bar!

Closure Scope

Closures have their own scope. A closure variable persists between calls to the closure. Use the `&lambda` function to create a new closure and initialize its values.

```
sub accum
{
   return lambda({
      $i = $i + $1;
      return $i;
   }, $i => $1);
}

$a = accum(3);
println("a: " . [$a: 1]);
println("a: " . [$a: 1]);

$b = accum(30);
println("b: " . [$b: 2]);
println("b: " . [$b: 2]);

println("a: " . [$a: 3]);
println("b: " . [$b: 3]);
```

```
a: 4
a: 5
b: 32
b: 34
a: 8
b: 37
```

This example shows a Sleep Accumulator Generator. An Accumulator Generator is a function that returns an accumulator function. The accumulator function contains an initial value and increments itself with each call by some parameter.

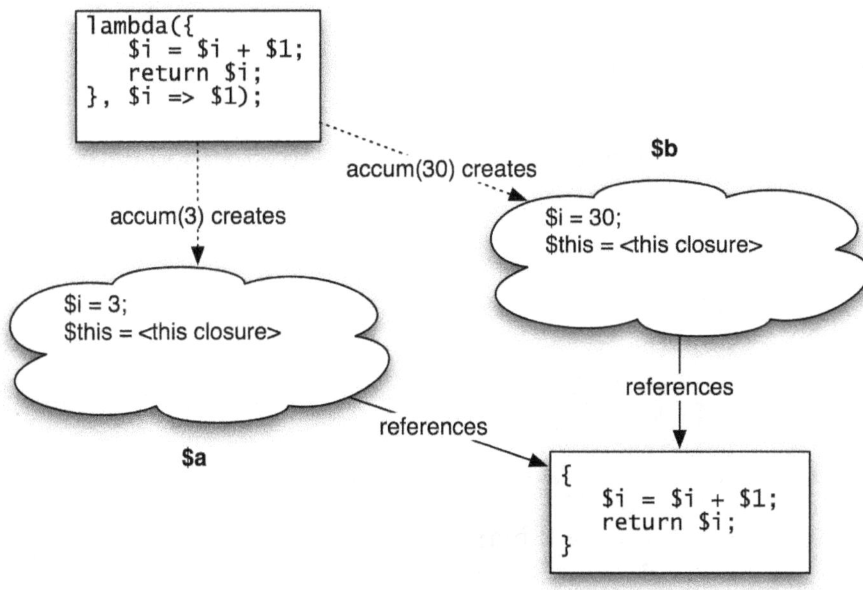

Each call to lambda creates a new closure. You can call and set values within these closures independent of other closures--even if they refer to the same code.

Use the `&this` function to place values into the scope of "this" closure.

```
$myfunc = {
   this('$a $b $c @array %hash');
   # do stuff...
};
```

Each closure contains the scalar *$this*. *$this* is a reference to the current closure.

Index Operator

Use the index operator to get a value from the this scope of a closure.

```
$closure = lambda({
                 println("\$x is $x");
              }, $x => 33);

[$closure];

$closure['$x'] = "test!";
[$closure];

println("Accessing a value: " . $closure['$x']);
```

```
$x is 33
$x is test!
Accessing a value: test!
```

Closures as Psuedo Objects

Object expressions accept a message parameter as *$0*. This is akin to a method name in a class.

```
$closure = {
   println("Message is $0 argument is $1");
};

[$closure foo: "bar"];
```

```
Message is foo argument is bar
```

This parameter allows you to create closures and manipulate them much like objects. This example shows a closure acting as a Stack object.

```
sub BuildStack
{
   return {
      this('@stack');
      if ($0 eq "push") { push(@stack, $1); }
      if ($0 eq "pop") { return pop(@stack); }
      if ($0 eq "isEmpty")
      {
         return iff(size(@stack) == 0, 1, 0);
      }
   };
}

$mystack = BuildStack();
[$mystack push: "apple"];
[$mystack push: "bananna"];
[$mystack push: "cat?!?"];

while (![$mystack isEmpty])
{
   println("Pop!: " . [$mystack pop]);
}
```

Pop!: cat?!?
Pop!: bananna
Pop!: apple

This example works much like the accumulator generator. Each call to `&BuildStack` generates a new closure.

Seriously, Sleep doesn't have classes and objects?

All of this discussion so far has lead to this. Seriously. Sleep doesn't have classes and objects. Sleep's closures are very powerful though. If you want a generic data structure that groups together data and functionality, try this on for size:

```
# everything you need for Sleep OO

sub object
{
   local('$function');

   $function = function("& $+ $type $+ :: $+ $0");
   if ($function !is $null)
   {
      return invoke($function, @_, $0, $this => $this);
   }
```

```
    throw "$type $+ :: $+ $0 - no such method";
}

sub newObject
{
    local('$object');
    $object = lambda(&object, $type => $1);

    # invoke the constructor
    invoke($object, sublist(@_, 1), "init", $this => $object);

    return $object;
}
```

The `&newObject` function creates a new closure from `&object` with a *$type* variable in its scope. The other arguments to `&newObject` are passed to `"& $+ $type $+ ::init"` which acts as a constructor. The constructor is invoked with the *$this* scope of the new closure.

The `&object` closure contains code for a generic method dispatcher. When invoked, it looks at *$0* and finds a method matching `"& $+ $type $+ :: $+ $0"`. If found, the method is invoked within the scope of the object closure instance.

You can think of the closure scope as a class scope.

Now that we can combine functions and data, let us discuss classes.

```
include("object.sl");

# define our person object

sub person::init
{
    this('$name $age');
    ($name, $age) = @_;
}

sub person::print
{
    println("Person: $name ( $+ $age yrs old)");
}

# use it

$raffi = newObject("person", "Raphael", 27);
[$raffi print];
```

```
$frances = newObject("person", "Frances", 26);
[$frances print];
```

Person: Raphael (27 yrs old)
Person: Frances (26 yrs old)

And that's all there is to it. Implementing inheritance and other object oriented features is left as an exercise to you dear reader.

Can I interoperate with Java this way?

This question is beyond the scope of this chapter. The short answer is--yes. Sleep has a feature to use closures as psuedo objects that respond to certain interfaces. This topic is covered in chapter 7.2 Proxy Instances.

Memoization

Chapter 3 introduced ordered hashes along with removal and miss policies. You can use the miss policy of an ordered hash to transparently enable a powerful optimization known as memoization. Memoization caches the results of a function call to prevent unnecessary calculations.

Here is a naive implementation of the Fibonacci sequence with runtime statistics.

```
sub fib
{
   if ($1 == 0)
   {
      return 0L;
   }
   else if ($1 == 1)
   {
      return 1L;
   }
   else
   {
      return fib($1 - 1) + fib($1 - 2);
   }
}

println("Fib no. " . fib(30L));
```

$ **java -jar sleep.jar --time fib2.sl**
Fib no. 832040
time: 50.368s

Not very fast is it? This naive implementation requires 2,692,537 recursive function calls to complete the computation.

This next function shows how to implement memoization in Sleep. This function accepts a closure argument and returns a memoized version of it.

```
sub memoize
{
   local('%cache');
   %cache = ohash();

   setMissPolicy(%cache,
      lambda(
         {
            # $2 is the requested key as provided
            return invoke($function, $2);
         }, $function => $1)
   );

   return lambda({ return %cache[@_]; }, \%cache);
}
```

How does it work? This function constructs an ordered hash. The miss policy of the ordered hash calls the function we want to memoize. The miss policy puts the return value of the function into the ordered hash.

Now we apply memoization to the Fibonacci program.

```
include("memoize.sl");

sub fib
{
   if ($1 == 0)
   {
      return 0L;
   }
   else if ($1 == 1)
   {
      return 1L;
   }
   else
   {
      return fib($1 - 1) + fib($1 - 2);
   }
}

setf('&fib', memoize(&fib));
```

```
println("Fib no. " . fib(30L));
```

```
$ java -jar sleep.jar --time fib1.sl
Fib no. 832040
time: 0.25s
```

As you can see the numbers are quite different this time. Memoization is not a catch-all though. Do not use memoization on functions that have side effects.

5.4 Continuations

Closures can pause their execution and call another function that does something with the paused closure. A paused closure is a continuation. Calling a paused closure resumes its execution.

When pausing a closure, Sleep saves the compiled code, call stack, program counter, local variables, and closure variables into a closure object.

To save a continuation use the `callcc` command and specify a function to call. Read `callcc` as: call the specified function with a continuation of the current function as an argument.

```
callcc &closure;
```

This example shows `callcc` with the producer and consumer problem.

```
$buffer  = $null;

sub produce
{
   for ($x = 0; $x < 3; $x++)
   {
      println("Produce: $x * 3");
      $buffer = $x * 3;
      callcc &consume;
   }
}

sub consume
{
   println("Consume: $buffer");
   [$1];  # resume the calling function
}

produce();
```

Produce: 0 * 3
Consume: 0
Produce: 1 * 3
Consume: 3
Produce: 2 * 3
Consume: 6

The producer pauses itself and sends control to the consumer function. The consume function consumes some data. It then invokes its first argument. Think of `callcc` as a functional goto with a rope to go back to the old function.

Example: Mobile Agents

Agent programming is a paradigm for distributed computing. An agent system is multiple independent actors executing asynchronous of one another. Clever programmers will create a generic template of functionality and customize each instance with various parameters on deployment. In this way you can gain a lot of functionality for very little code.

An agent system requires a means to implement the agents themselves and middleware to execute the agents within. Here is a closure implementation of an agent:

```
sub InfoAgent
{
   local('$user');

   $user = systemProperties()["user.name"];
   println("1) I am $user");

   move($destination);

   println("2) On $source I am $user");
   $user = systemProperties()["user.name"];
   println("2) Here I am $user");

   move($source);

   println("3) Back home, I was $user");
}
```

You may notice the `&move` function. This is the agent requesting to move to another computer. Agents that can relocate themselves are mobile agents. `&move` is an inline function hiding a `callcc` that calls `sendAgent` with the desired host and continuation.

```
inline move
{
   callcc lambda(
```

```
    {
       sendAgent($host, $1);
    }, $host => $1);
}
```

The &sendAgent function is shown below. Serialization allows scripts to persist and reconstitute scalars to and from any I/O channel. Sleep uses serialization to write and read continuations to and from a socket.

```
# sendAgent("host", $continuation)
sub sendAgent
{
   local('$handle');
   $handle = connect($1, 8888);
   writeObject($handle, $2);
   closef($handle);
}
```

The server for the &sendAgent function is the middleware for the Sleep agents. This server is a loop that listens for a connection, reads an object, and creates an isolated thread that executes the read-in object.

```
while (1)
{
   $handle = listen(8888, 0);
   $agent = readObject($handle);
   closef($handle);

   fork({ [$agent]; }, \$agent);
}
```

With these pieces in place, the final step is to launch the agent into the system:

```
$agent = lambda(&InfoAgent,
                  $source => "sleep.dashnine.org",
                  $destination => "apollo.ecs.syr.edu");
sendAgent("sleep.dashnine.org", $agent);
```

[raffi@dashnine ~]$ **java -jar sleep.jar launch.sl**

apollo 185: **java -jar sleep.jar mw.sl**
2) On sleep.dashnine.org I am raffi
2) Here I am rmudge

[raffi@dashnine ~]$ **java -jar sleep.jar mw.sl**
1) I am raffi
3) Back home, I was rmudge

To execute this example include the `&move` and `&sendAgent` functions in your mw.sl and launch.sl files.

Coroutines

Use the the `yield` command to pause a closure. `yield` can give back a value like `return`. A coroutine is a function that is paused with `yield`.

yield `expression;`

Coroutines allow elegant solutions to problems that require recursion and tracking state.

The return command discards the state of a coroutine. State is discarded when the function ends.

Sleep coroutines can call themselves or eachother recursively.

Generators with Coroutines

A generator is a function that generates a sequence. Coroutines are natural for implementing generators.

```
sub range
{
   # Returns a new function that returns the next number in the
   # range with each call.  Returns $null at the end of the range

   return lambda(
   {
      local('$counter');
      for ($counter = $begin; $counter <= $end; $counter++)
      {
         yield $counter;
      }
   }, $begin => $1, $end => $2);
}
```

This example implements a range function that returns a generator. I use a foreach loop to iterate over the generator.

```
foreach $value (range(8, 13))
{
   println($value);
}
```

```
8
9
10
11
12
13
```

Example: List Co-iteration

This example iterates over two arrays with a generator and an assignment loop.

```
sub both
{
   local('$a $b');
   ($a, $b) = @_;

   while (size($a) > 0 || size($b) > 0)
   {
      # yield the heads of our lists
      yield @($a[0], $b[0]);

      # set the lists to the rest values
      $a = sublist($a, 1);
      $b = sublist($b, 1);
   }
}

@a = @("a", "b", "c", "d");
@b = @(1, 2, 3);

while @items (both(@a, @b))
{
   ($x, $y) = @items;
   println("$x and $y");
}
```

```
a and 1
b and 2
c and 3
d and
```

Each iteration through the `&both` function returns the head (first element) of the two lists stored in it. The heads of the two lists are then set to the sublist consisting of all elements from the second element to the end of the list.

Example: Tree Traversal

You can use coroutines to traverse through graph and tree data structures.

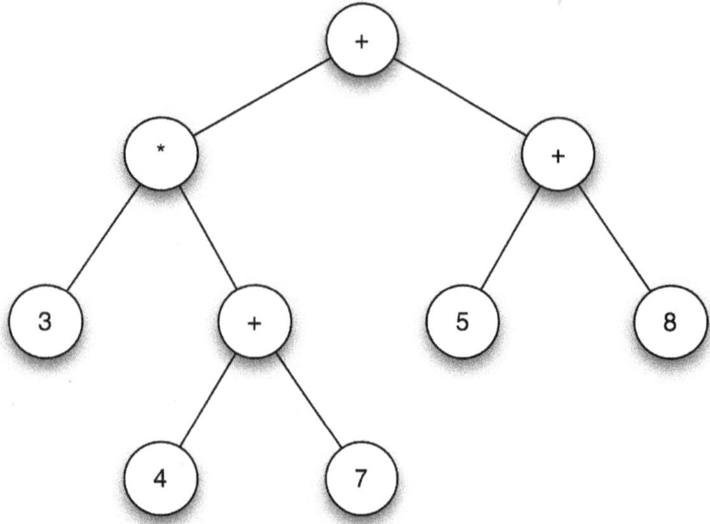

This example is an interpreter that uses a preorder traversal of the pictured expression tree. Compilers generate an expression tree and walk it in this way to generate or interpret code.

```
# Represent a tree as a hashmap with the following values:
#   left - left branch;
#   right - right branch;
#   label - label for this portion

# this function returns a tree:
sub n
{
   return %(label => $1, left => $2, right => $3);
}

# do a preorder traversal of a tree..
sub preorder
{
   local('$x');

   if (-ishash $1)
   {
      while $x (preorder($1["left"]))
      {
         yield $x;
      }
```

```
      while $x (preorder($1["right"]))
      {
         yield $x;
      }

      yield $1["label"];
   }
   else
   {
      yield $1;
   }

   return $null;
}

# create an expression tree for: (3 * (4 + 7)) + (5 + 8)

$tree = n("+", n("*", 3, n("+", 4, 7)), n("+", 5, 8));

# evaluate the expression tree...:
while $node (preorder($tree))
{
   if (-isnumber $node)
   {
      push(@stack, $node);
      println("push $node");
   }
   else
   {
      $b = pop(@stack);
      $a = pop(@stack);

      push(@stack, expr("$a $node $b"));
      println("oper $node [ $+ $a $+ , $b $+ ]: " . @stack[-1]);
   }
}

println("Final answer: " . @stack[0]);
```

```
push 3
push 4
push 7
oper + [4, 7]: 11
oper * [3, 11]: 33
push 5
push 8
oper + [5, 8]: 13
```

oper + [33, 13]: 46
Final answer: 46

6. Regular Expressions

6.1 The Matcher

This quote from Jamie Zawinski summarizes everything you need to know about regular expressions.

```
"Some people, when confronted with a problem, think 'I
know, I'll use regular expressions.' Now they have two
problems."
```

Do you still want to read this chapter? Regular expressions are good to know. They can help you parse strings without having to write much code. Regular expressions are their own language that specify the make-up of an acceptable string. A matcher applies a regular expression pattern to a string to check for a match and to extract substrings.

In Sleep `ismatch` and `hasmatch` functions use regular expressions to check if a string matches a pattern. The function `&matches` extracts substrings based on the results of a pattern applied to a string. The function `&replace` uses regular expressions to specify patterns of text to replace. And the function `&split` uses a regular expression as the delimeter for breaking a string into several pieces.

All of this functionality uses the same underlying matcher engine. Before use the regular expression engine compiles the pattern into a state machine. The matcher then starts at the beginning of the state machine and at the beginning of your string. The matcher consumes characters from the input string until it satisfies the current state. It then tries to satisfy the next state in the state machine. The matcher "backtracks" to a previous state with another potential path when it cannot satisfy the current state. A successful match will consume the entire string and end in a success state of the pattern. The string is a non-match when these conditions aren't met.

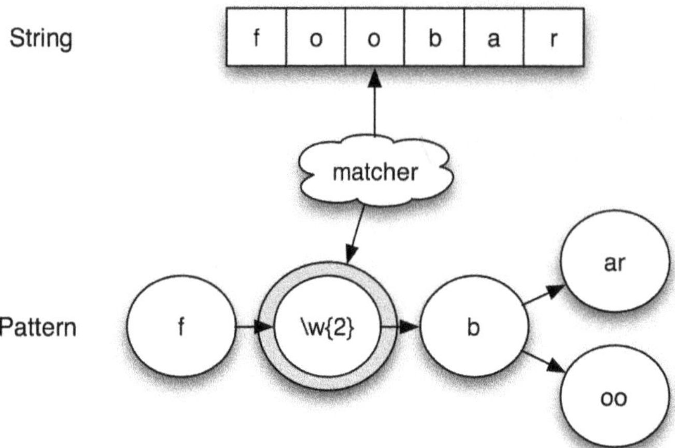

This diagram shows the string "foobar" applied to the pattern 'f\w{2}b(ar|oo)'. This pattern matches any string that begins with "f", followed by 2 letters, followed by a "b", followed by "ar" or "oo". The arrow to from the matcher to the string represents the current string location. The arrow from the matcher to the \w{2} state represents the current pattern element.

6.2 Pattern Elements

There are several constructs within the regular expression language you should be aware of. Pattern elements represent a set of one or more acceptable characters. Pattern elements are literal characters, character classes, and groups. Groups consist of regular expression patterns sometimes with special options or logical operators. Quantifiers repeat a pattern element a fixed or variable number of times.

Literal Characters

Literal characters are the simplest pattern element. The pattern 'a' matches the string "a". The pattern 'ardvark' matches the string "ardvark". Literal characters specify the only character that the matcher will accept from the current string location.

These sequences describe literal characters:

Sequence	Meaning
a	Matches the character a
\\	Matches the backslash character

Sequence	Meaning
`\0n`	Matches the character at octal value n
`\0nn`	Matches the character at octal value nn
`\0mnn`	Matches the character at octal value mnn
`\xhh`	Matches the character at hexadecimal value 0xhh
`\uhhhh`	Matches the character at hexadecimal value 0xhhhh
`\t`	Matches the tab character
`\n`	Matches the line feed character
`\r`	Matches the carriage-return character
`\f`	Matches the form-feed character
`\a`	Matches the alert (bell) character
`\e`	Matches the escape character
`\cx`	Matches the control character x

The `ismatch` predicate returns true if the pattern describes the string.

```
$ java -jar sleep.jar
>> Welcome to the Sleep scripting language
> ? "this is a test" ismatch 'this is a test'
true
> ? "abcd" ismatch 'abce'
false
> ? "abcd" ismatch '\x61\x62\x63\x64'
true
> ? "abcd" ismatch '\u0061\x62\x63\x64'
true
```

Why should I use single quoted strings for patterns?

The matcher interprets the string it receives as the pattern. To match a single `\`, the regex engine requires the `\\` sequence. Single and double quoted strings process `'\\\\'` to `'\\'`. Double quoted strings associate special meaning with many escaped characters. Single quoted strings have meanings for `'\\'` and `'\''` only. Using single quoted strings you avoid surprises.

The `&split` function uses a regular expression pattern as the delimeter for breaking a string into pieces.

```
@data = @("Raphael,Professional Escort,NY",
          "Frances,Sales Warrior,MI");

foreach $var (@data)
{
```

```
    ($name, $job, $state) = split(',', $var);
    println("$name works as a $job in $state");
}
```

Raphael works as a Professional Escort in NY
Frances works as a Sales Warrior in MI

Regular expression patterns are full of characters that have special meanings. Quote a character to force a literal match.

Sequence	Meaning
`\`	Quotes the next character
`\Q`	Begins a quote sequence
`\E`	Ends a quote sequence

A quote sequence quotes all characters within it.

```
> ? '\x62' ismatch '\\\\x62'
true
> ? "\x62" ismatch '\\\\x62'
false
> ? '\t\n' ismatch '\Q\t\n\E'
true
> ? "\t\n" ismatch '\Q\t\n\E'
false
```

Custom Character Classes

Literal characters produce matchers that can match only one string. You have to use character classes to match more than one string. A character class represents the set of all characters that the matcher will accept from the current string location.

Enclose a custom character class with square brackets. It is a common to confuse character classes with groups. Character classes match a single character. A group matches a sequence of characters.

A custom character class:

- may contain a range of characters or numbers.
- may contain other custom character classes--this expands what the class accepts
- negates itself when it begins with a ^
- uses && to combine acceptance criteria from another custom character class

Sequence	Meaning
`[abc]`	Matches a, b, or c

Sequence	Meaning
`[c-m]`	Matches any character c through m
`[ab[xy]]`	Matches a, b, x, or y
`[^0-9]`	Matches any non-digit
`[a-m&&[bar]`	Matches a or b
`[a-z&&[^w-y]`	Matches a through z except for w, x, and y.

Examples:

```
> ? "r" ismatch '[bar]'
true
> ? "bar" ismatch '[bar]'
false
> ? "34a" ismatch '[0-9][0-9][a-z]'
true
> ? "34A" ismatch '[0-9][0-9][a-z]'
false
```

Built-in Character Classes

Several built-in character classes exist. These save you the trouble of defining custom character classes.

Sequence	Meaning
`.`	Matches anything
`\d`	Matches any digit 0-9
`\D`	Matches any non-digit
`\s`	Matches any whitespace character
`\S`	Matches any non-whitespace character
`\w`	Matches any word character (a-z, A-Z, _, and 0-9)
`\W`	Matches any non-word character

For historical reasons, POSIX character classes exist as well.

Sequence	Meaning
`\p{Lower}`	Matches a lower-case letter
`\p{Upper}`	Matches an upper-case letter
`\p{ASCII}`	Matches all ASCII characters
`\p{Alpha}`	Matches a letter
`\p{Digit}`	Matches a digit 0-9
`\p{Alnum}`	Matches a number or letter
`\p{Punct}`	Matches one of !"#$%&'()*+,-./:;?@[\]^_`{|}~

Sequence	Meaning
`\p{Graph}`	Matches a number, letter, or punctuation character
`\p{Print}`	Matches a printable character. Same as \p{Graph}
`\p{Blank}`	Matches a space or a tab
`\p{Cntrl}`	Matches a control character
`\p{XDigit}`	Matches a hexadecimal digit
`\p{Space}`	Matches a whitespace character

Sleep patterns can use blocks and categories from the Unicode specification. See http://unicode.org/reports/tr18/ for more information.

Sequence	Meaning
`\p{InGreek}`	Matches a character in the Greek block (simple block)
`\p{Lu}`	Matches an uppercase letter (simple category)
`\p{Sc}`	Matches a currency symbol

You may negate posix class definitions with an uppercase `\P`:

Sequence	Meaning
`\P{ASCII}`	Matches anything except ASCII characters
`[\p{Space}&&\P{Blank}]`	Matches any whitespace except for a space or a tab

Examples:

```
> ? "X" ismatch '.'
true
> ? "\x00" ismatch '.'
true
> ? "34" ismatch '\d\d'
true
> ? "E4" ismatch '\d\d'
false
> ? '$33' ismatch '\p{Sc}\d\d'
true
```

Groups

A group encloses one or more pattern elements with parentheses. A group represents a sequence of pattern elements that the matcher must accept from the current string location.

The pipe character specifies alternate acceptable patterns. `'foo|bar'` matches the strings `"foo"` or `"bar"`. The alternation operator can lead to slow matcher performance. Avoid it if possible.

Sequence	Meaning
`XY`	Matches X followed by Y
`X|Y`	Matches the sequence X or Y

Examples:

```
> ? "foobar" ismatch 'f\w\wb(ar|oo)'
true
> ? "fayboo" ismatch 'f\w\wb(ar|oo)'
true
> ? "foobor" ismatch 'f\w\wb(ar|oo)'
false
```

All groups are capture groups by default. Capture groups are numbered from 1 to n by counting the opening parentheses from left to right. Group 0 represents the entire match.

The matcher saves matched substrings during processing. The matcher tracks substrings by capture group. You can use a backreference to recall a capture group. A backreference is the backslash character followed by a capture group number. As an example, `'(foo|bar)\1'` matches `"foofoo"` or `"barbar"` but not `"foobar"` or `"barfoo"`. The `\1` in the pattern recalls of the text from the first capture group.

A group prefixed with a question mark and a colon is a non-capturing group. These groups do not save substrings and do not affect the capture group count.

Sequence	Meaning
`(?:X)`	Matches X as a non-capturing group
`(X)`	Matches X as a capturing group
`\n`	Matches whatever the nth capturing group matched

The `&matched` function returns the matches from the last `ismatch` or `hasmatch` comparison.

```
if ("(654) 555-1212" ismatch '\((\d\d\d)\) (\d\d\d-\d\d\d\d)')
{
   ($areaCode, $phoneNumber) = matched();
   println("dial 1 and $areaCode before $phoneNumber");
}
```

dial 1 and 654 before 555-1212

As a shortcut, the `&matches` function carries out the comparison and extraction operations in one call.

```
# trim whitespace from start of a string
$trimmed = matches("\t   this is a test", '\s*(.*)')[0];
println($trimmed);
```

this is a test

The `&replace` function recalls capture group elements as well. The literal values `'$1'` .. `'$n'` in the replacement value are substituted for the recalled text. This example changes bold html tags to underline:

```
$bold = 'This string has <b>bolded</b> text and <b>lots of it</b> :)';
$underline = replace($bold, '<b>(.*?)</b>', "<u>\$1</u>");
println($underline);
```

This string has <u>bolded</u> text and <u>lots of it</u> :)

The `ismatch` predicate anchors itself to the beginning and end of a string by default. The cousin to `ismatch` is the `hasmatch` predicate. `hasmatch` looks for a substring within the string that satisfies the specified pattern. Moreover this predicate remembers the last substring it matched. Subsequent calls to `hasmatch` will return the next matching substring until no more matching substrings exist. At this point `hasmatch` returns false and clears its state information.

```
sub printDocumentTree
{
   local('$tag $content');

   while ($1 hasmatch '<(.*?)>(.*?)</\1>')
   {
      ($tag, $content) = matched();
      println(("   " x $2) . "+- $tag $+ : $content");
      printDocumentTree($content, $2 + 1);
   }
}

$html = "<html><title>Hello World!</title><p>It's a <b>nice</b>
day</p></html>";
printDocumentTree($html, 0);
```

+- html: <title>Hello World!</title><p>It's a <b>nice</b> day</p>
   +- title: Hello World!
   +- p: It's a <b>nice</b> day
      +- b: nice

6.3 Quantifiers

So far we have seen patterns that accept a fixed length string. To match two digits requires `'\d\d'`. Literal characters and character classes let you specify what to match. Can you construct a pattern to match 2-3 digits? With what I've shown you so far, you can't.

The specification of how many is left to quantifiers. Quantifiers attach a repetition quantity to pattern elements. This quantity specifies how many times an element can repeat.

The following table shows the available quantifiers.

Sequence	Meaning
`X?`	Matches X once or not at all
`X*`	Matches X zero or more times
`X+`	Matches X one or more times
`X{n}`	Matches X exactly n times
`X{n,}`	Matches X at least n times
`X{n,m}`	Matches X at least n but no more than m times

Examples:

```
> ? "ooooooooh yeah!" ismatch 'o+h yeah!'
true
> ? "0o0o0o0h yeah!" ismatch '[o0]+h yeah!'
true
> ? "89 bottles of beer on the wall" ismatch '\d{1,2} bottles of beer on the wall'
true
> ? "100 bottles of beer on the wall" ismatch '\d{1,2} bottles of beer on the wall'
false
> ? "" ismatch '.*'
true
```

Quantifiers consume characters in a greedy manner by default. A greedy quantifier will consume as many characters as possible before moving on to the next pattern element. If a match fails and a greedy quantifier is present, the matcher will backtrack and have the greedy quantifier give back a character. The matcher will then try to complete the match. If this fails it will go back to the greedy quantifier and ask for a character again. The matcher repeats this process until it accepts the string or there are no characters left to give back.

```
> ? '123456' ismatch '(\d+)(\d+)'
true
> x matches('123456', '(\d+)(\d+)')
@('12345', '6')
```

A possessive quantifier will consume as much of the string as possible. Possessive quantifiers differ from greedy quantifiers in how they respond to a match failure. A possessive quantifier will not give back characters like a greedy quantifier does. This will cause some matches that succeed with a greedy strategy to fail. The tradeoff is possessive quantifiers fail much faster than greedy quantifiers. Append a plus to make a quantifier use a possessive strategy.

```
> ? '123456' ismatch '(\d++)(\d++)'
false
```

A relucant quantifier will consume as few characters as possible before moving to the next pattern element. Append a question mark to make a quantifier use a reluctant strategy.

```
> x matches('123456', '(\d+?)(\d+)')
@('1', '23456')
```

6.4 Special Constructs

Look Arounds

A look around construct is a means to ask prequalifying questions about the rest of the input string before continuing with the match. Look arounds do not consume characters.

These constructs are summarized here:

Sequence	Meaning
(?=X)	Checks for X to occur later
(?!X)	Checks that X does not occur later
(?	Checks that X has occured
(?	Checks that X has not occured
(?>X)	Checks for X

An example:

```
if ('http://www.google.com/' ismatch '(?=http://)(.*)')
{
   ($url) = matched();
   println($url);
}
```

```
http://www.google.com/
```

Notice that the `http://` portion of the pattern is not consumed. It is merely a precondition for the matcher to continue matching the rest of the string.

Boundary Matchers

`hasmatch`, `&replace`, and other regex functionality do not anchor themselves to specific portions of a string. Boundary matchers exist to allow a pattern to anchor itself. The boundary matchers for pattern anchoring are listed below:

Sequence	Meaning
`^`	Matches the beginning of a line
`$`	Matches the end of a line
`\b`	Matches a word boundary
`\B`	Matches a non-word boundary
`\A`	Matches the beginning of the input
`\G`	Matches the end of the previous match
`\Z`	Matches the end of the input but for the final terminator, if any
`\z`	Matches the end of the input

This example uses `&replace` to replace instances of foo or bar only if they occur at the beginning of a string:

```
$string = replace("foo is the word, not bar!", '\Afoo|\Abar', "pHEAR");
println($string);
```

pHEAR is the word, not bar!

Matcher Options

The matcher engine is tweakable with a few parameters. These options are enabled and disabled as specified in the table:

Sequence	Meaning
`(?idm-sux)`	Sets matcher options [on: idm] [off: sux]
`(?ids-mu:X)`	Sets matcher options in a non-capturing group: [on: ids] [off: mu]

The option:

- `i` makes pattern matching case insensitive for ASCII characters
- `u` sets case insensitive matching for Unicode characters
- `d` option enables UNIX lines mode. This mode forces the matcher to recognize only `"\n"` as a new line
- `m` option enables multiline mode which makes the `^` and `$` boundary matchers match at the beginning/end of each line
- `s` flag allows the `.` built-in class to match any character including new lines

- x option forces the matcher to ignore white space and allow pattern comments. Pattern comments begin with a pound sign. and end with a newline.

```
$pattern = '(?x)          # ignore whitespace and enable comments
            (?=http://)   # look ahead for http:// first
            (.*)          # put the string into a capture group';

if ("http://sleep.dashnine.org/" ismatch $pattern)
{
   ($url) = matched();
   println($url);
}
```

http://sleep.dashnine.org/

7. Java Objects

7.1 Object Expressions

Sleep can create, access, and query Java objects through Object expressions. Converting Java programs to Sleep is a snap once you master the concepts in this chapter.

Object expressions are enclosed inside of square brackets. The first parameter of an object expression is a target. The second is the message. Sleep converts the return value of an object expression to a Sleep scalar.

[*target message*]

Use a *$scalar*, Java class, or other object expression as the target.

Object expressions can receive arguments. Specify arguments as a comma separated list separated from the target and message parameters by a colon.

[*target message*: *argument*, *argument*, ...]

Use object expressions to access the Java class library. A good first example is the famous `"Hello World"` program.

```
[[System out] println: "Hello World!"];
```

Hello World!

The target of this expression is `[System out]`. The message is `println`. And the argument is `"Hello World"`. Notice that `[System out]` is itself an object expression.

Messages are Java method and field names. A common mistake is to specify a field using the Java dot notation i.e.

```
[System.out println: "Hello World!"];
```

```
Error: Unknown expression at line 1
    out
Error: Unknown expression at line 1
    System
```

As you can see, this doesn't work.

You can use the Java dot notation to specify the full name of a class.

```
[[java.lang.System out] println: "Hello World!"];
```

```
Hello World!
```

Access named inner classes with a dollar sign between the parent and inner class names: `ParentClass$InnerClass`.

Scalars as Objects

All Sleep scalars have an object representation. You can use object expressions to operate on scalar data as well as Java data.

```
$value = ["this is a String" lastIndexOf: "i" ];
```

This example is equivalent to `"this is a string".lastIndexOf("i")` in Java. Numbers are treated as their wrapper java objects. For example: An object expression converts a double scalar into a `java.lang.Double` object.

```
$value = [3.45 isNaN];
```

Object Instantiation

Use the `new` keyword to instantiate an object. The syntax for this is:

`[new` *ClassName*`]` and `[new` *ClassName*`:` *argument*`,` *...*`]`.

An example:

```
$scalar = [new java.util.StringTokenizer: "this is a test", " "];
```

Sleep can import classes to save typing the package name each time. Sleep attempts to resolve literal class names against the import list at compile time.

```
import java.awt.Point;

$point = [new Point: 3, 4];
println($point);
```

```
java.awt.Point[x=3,y=4]
```

You can use wildcards to import the entire contents of a package.

```
import java.awt.*;
```

Sleep imports *java.lang*, *java.util*, and *sleep.runtime* by default.

Fields

Use the `&setField` function to set a field in an object to some value.

```
import java.awt.Point;

$p = [new Point];
setField($p, x => 33, y => 45);
println($p);
```

```
java.awt.Point[x=33,y=45]
```

Class Literals

The literal form for a `java.lang.Class` object in Sleep is the hat symbol followed by a classname. The parser resolves these literals when compiling the script.

The literal `^String` is equivalent to `[Class forName: "java.lang.String"]`.

Use the `isa` predicate to check if an object is an instance of a specified class:

```
>> Welcome to the Sleep scripting language
> ? "some string" isa ^String
true
> ? 33.0 isa ^String
false
> ? 33.0 isa ^Double
true
```

3rd-party Jars

Sleep can dynamically import packages from jar files that do not currently exist on the Java classpath. Use an import from statement:

import *package* from: *path-to/filename.jar*;

This snippet uses the JDOM XML API located in jdom.jar:

```
import org.jdom.*         from: jdom.jar;
import org.jdom.input.*   from: jdom.jar;
import org.jdom.output.* from: jdom.jar;

# load the document in
$builder  = [new SAXBuilder];
$document = [$builder build: @ARGV[0]];

# print the document out.
$output   = [new XMLOutputter: [Format getPrettyFormat]];
[$output output: $document, [System out]];
```

Sleep has its own classpath (the current working directory is included). The import from statement will attempt to find the jar file in any of the Sleep classpath folders. Read the Sleep classpath value with `systemProperties()["sleep.classpath"]`. Setting the Sleep classpath is covered in chapter 1.

Taint Mode and Objects

Taint mode is a security feature of Sleep that flags all data originating from an external source as tainted. Data derived from tainted data is considered tainted as well. Some functions will not accept tainted data in their arguments. Sensitive functions include `&compile_closure`, `&eval`, `&expr`, and `&include`.

Sleep will taint objects that receive tainted arguments in an object expression. Object expressions that query a tainted object will return tainted data. This is excessive but it gets the job done.

```
debug(debug() | 128);

import java.util.LinkedList;

$evals = [new LinkedList];
[$evals add: "2 + 2"];
[$evals add: @ARGV[0]];

$iterator = [$evals iterator];
```

```
while ([$iterator hasNext])
{
   $next = [$iterator next];
   println("$next = " . expr($next));
}
```

```
$ java -Dsleep.taint=true -jar sleep.jar taint2.sl "3 * 9"
Warning: tainted object: [2 + 2] from: '3 * 9' at taint2.sl:7
Warning: tainted value: 1 from: '3 * 9' at taint2.sl:7
Warning: tainted value: java.util.LinkedList$ListItr@199939 from: [2 + 2, 3 * 9] at taint2.sl:9
Warning: tainted value: 1 from: java.util.LinkedList$ListItr@199939 at taint2.sl:10
Warning: tainted value: '2 + 2' from: java.util.LinkedList$ListItr@199939 at taint2.sl:12
Warning: Insecure &expr: '2 + 2' is tainted at taint2.sl:13
Warning: tainted value: 1 from: java.util.LinkedList$ListItr@199939 at taint2.sl:10
Warning: tainted value: '3 * 9' from: java.util.LinkedList$ListItr@199939 at taint2.sl:12
Warning: Insecure &expr: '3 * 9' is tainted at taint2.sl:13
Warning: tainted value: 0 from: java.util.LinkedList$ListItr@199939 at taint2.sl:10
```

To detaint a Sleep scalar use `&untaint`. Use `&debug` level 128 to trace the propagation of tainted values. To enable/disable this mode see 1.1 Stand-alone Scripts: Command Line Options.

See Chapter 9.3 Extend Sleep: Taint Mode for more background on taint mode.

Parameter Marshalling

Object expressions that send messages to Java objects must resolve the proper method to use. Sleep employs a heuristic to map scalar types to Java types.

This heuristic loops through all methods with the same name as the message parameter. The algorithm checks each method signatuare against the expression arguments looking for a best match.

In general a match is determined by checking if the scalar type is an instance of the expected Java object. Sleep's primitive types (int, double, long) map to their equivalent Java primitive types.

Sleep converts arrays to a `java.util.Collection` and hashes to a `java.util.Map`.

Sleep also makes an effort to convert Sleep arrays to Java arrays if necessary. The interpreter uses the first element of the Sleep array to determine the type of the Java array.

Closures are automatically marshalled into proxy object instances. I describe this process in the next subsection.

$null maps to *null* automatically.

The following table details the definite match and secondary match for Sleep types mapping to Java types:

Scalar Type	Primary Match	Secondary Match
string		
	java.lang.String char (length == 1)	char[] byte[] java.lang.Object
int		
	int	java.lang.Integer *other primitives* java.lang.Object java.lang.String
double		
	double	java.lang.Double *other primitives* java.lang.Object java.lang.String
long		
	long	java.lang.Long *other primitives* java.lang.Object java.lang.String
object		
	anything I am an instanceof	
&closure		
	Any Java interface	java.lang.Object
@array		
	java array java.util.List java.util.Collection sleep.runtime.ScalarArray	java.lang.Object
%hash		
	java.util.Map sleep.runtime.ScalarHash	java.lang.Object
$null		
	matches everything :)	

You can bypass this automatic marshalling with casting. Individual scalars are cast using the `&casti` function.

```
$cast = casti(1, 'b');
println([$cast getClass]);
```

```
$cast = casti(33.5, 'f');
println([$cast getClass]);
```

class java.lang.Byte
class java.lang.Float

Create Java arrays of any dimension and type with the `&cast` function.

```
@array = @("a", "b", "c", "d", "e", "f");
$casted = cast(@array, "*", 2, 3); # create a 2x3 array

println("Class is: " . [$casted getClass]);
```

Class is: class [[Ljava.lang.String;

Values returned by object expressions are marshalled back into scalar types. This process is detailed in the following table:

Java Types	Scalar Types
boolean / java.lang.Boolean (*false*)	*$null*
boolean / java.lang.Boolean (*true*)	int
byte / java.lang.Byte	int
byte[]	string
char / java.lang.Character	string
char[]	string
double / java.lang.Double	double
float / java.lang.Float	double
int / java.lang.Integer	int
java.lang.Array	*@array*
java.lang.Object	object
java.lang.String	string
long / java.lang.Long	long
null	*$null*
short / java.lang.Short	int

Use `&scalar` to feed an object scalar through this conversion process.

7.2 Proxy Instances

Sleep can convert a closure into an anonymous Java object that responds to certain interfaces. This object is a proxy instance. The interpreter automatically marshalls closures to proxy instances when passing them to Java.

This feature works only on interfaces right now. In the future there may be an addon that allows this with arbitrary Java objects.

A Java method call on a proxy instance results in a call on a closure. The argument *$0* is set to the method name. The arguments from Java are converted to scalars *$1, $2,* etc.

```
debug(7);
global('$frame $button $clicked');

import javax.swing.*;
import java.awt.*;

$frame = [new JFrame: "Test"];
[$frame setSize: 240, 120];
[$frame setDefaultCloseOperation: [JFrame EXIT_ON_CLOSE]];

$button = [new JButton: "Click me"];

[[$frame getContentPane] add: $button];

[$frame show];

$clicked = 0;

sub button_pressed {
   # $0 is "actionPerformed"
   # $1 is a java.awt.event.ActionEvent object

   $clicked++;

   [[$1 getSource] setText: "Clicked $clicked time(s)"];
}

# add &button_pressed as our action listener

[$button addActionListener: &button_pressed];
```

A screenshot of the application:

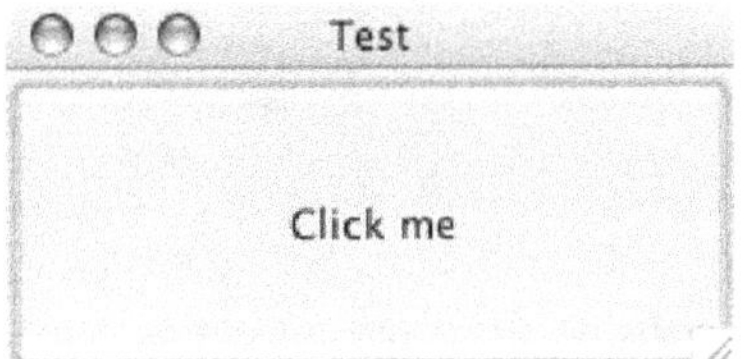

This example marshalls `&button_pressed` into a `java.awt.event.ActionListener` instance. Any call to `actionPerformed` calls `&button_pressed` with *$0* set to `actionPerformed` and *$1* set to the `java.awt.event.ActionEvent` object.

Uncaught exceptions within a proxy instance will bubble up to the calling Java object. Sleep wraps a non-throwable object with a `java.lang.RuntimeException`.

```
debug(7);
global('$frame $button');

import javax.swing.*;
import java.awt.*;

$frame = [new JFrame: "Test Exceptions"];
[$frame setSize: 240, 120];
[$frame setDefaultCloseOperation: [JFrame EXIT_ON_CLOSE]];

$button = [new JButton: "Click me"];

[[$frame getContentPane] add: $button];

[$frame show];

sub button_pressed {
   throw "argh, why did you click me?";
}

[$button addActionListener: &button_pressed];
```

Exception in thread "AWT-EventQueue-0" java.lang.RuntimeException: argh, why did you click me?

Create proxy instances with the `&newInstance` function.

7.3 Exceptions

Exceptions that come from Java are soft errors. You can use the `&checkError` mechanism to retrieve them.

```
import sleep.error.YourCodeSucksException;

$loader = [new ScriptLoader];
$script = [$loader loadScript: "debunked.sl"];

if (checkError($exception))
{
   if ($exception isa ^YourCodeSucksException)
   {
      print([$exception formatErrors]);
   }
}
else
{
   [$script runScript];
}
```

```
Error: Mismatched Parentheses - missing close paren at line 2
     println($x;
            ^
```

Or if you set `&debug` 34 you can use try catch blocks to respond to exceptions. See 4.3 Exceptions: Choice in Error Handling for more details.

```
import sleep.error.YourCodeSucksException;

debug(debug() | 34); # throw all soft errors

try
{
   $loader = [new ScriptLoader];
   $script = [$loader loadScript: "debunked.sl"];
   [$script runScript];
}
catch $exception
{
   if ($exception isa ^YourCodeSucksException)
   {
      print([$exception formatErrors]);
   }
}
```

```
Error: Mismatched Parentheses - missing close paren at line 2
     println($x;
            ^
```

8. Input / Output

8.1 I/O Handles

Sleep scripts can interact with a multitude of I/O sources. Open operations return an object scalar that references a `sleep.bridges.io.IOObject`. Through this chapter I refer to an `IOObject` as a handle. You can read, write, and manipulate a handle with Sleep's I/O library.

Files

To open a file, in read mode, and print its contents line by line:

```
$handle = openf("/etc/passwd");

while $text (readln($handle))
{
   println("Read: $text");
}
```

The `&openf` function returns an I/O handle. The assignment loop reads the contents of the file. Most read functions return *$null* when there is no data left. This makes assignment loops a great tool for iterating the contents of a handle.

The `&openf` function can append to or overwrite a file. Prefix the filename with a `>` to specify overwrite or a `>>` to specify append. These character sequences have the same meaning as redirect operators in UNIX and Windows command shells.

```
# overwrite data.txt

$handle = openf(">data.txt");
println($handle, "this is some data.");
closef($handle);
```

This example overwrites the contents of data.txt. At the end of the script, `&closef` closes the handle. `&closef` is the universal function for closing any I/O source.

Query the open or closed state of a handle with the end-of-file (`-eof`) predicate.

```
$handle = openf("/etc/passwd");
# do something...
closef($handle);

if (-eof $handle)
{
   println("handle is closed!");
}
```

handle is closed!

I/O Errors

Read, write, and open errors are available with `&checkError`.

```
$handle = openf("fjkdfdjkslgds");

if (checkError($error))
{
   println("Could not open file: $error");
}
```

Could not open file: java.io.FileNotFoundException: /Users/raffi/manual/manual/fjkdfdjkslgds (No such file or directory)

I/O failures are soft errors. They are silent unless you place a `&checkError` after each call or set `&debug` level 2 to print errors as they occur.

Data Integrity

Scripts can assure the integrity of data across a stream by calculating a checksum or cryptographic digest. To calculate a digest or checksum on a handle use the `&digest` or `&checksum` functions before reading (or writing) data.

```
# generate an MD5 digest of any file.
```

```
sub md5
{
   $handle = openf($1);
   $digest = digest($handle, "MD5");

   # consume the handle
   skip($handle, lof($1));

   closef($handle);

   $result = unpack("H*", digest($digest))[0];
   println("MD5 ( $+ $1 $+ ) = $result");
}

md5(@ARGV[0]);
```

MD5 (digest.sl) = ff4ddf4a2006140f8db28904de9e288b

This example is a generic function that mimics the UNIX `md5` command. This script calls `&digest` in 2 different contexts. The first call sets up the digest and specifies the algorithm. The second call gets the bytes representing the MD5 digest of all data that traversed through the handle.

Filesystem

Operating systems vary in their choice of path separation character. Sleep uses the forward slash as a universal separation character. I/O functions substitute the forward slash for the platform specific separation character in filenames.

Sleep keeps track of the current working directory of a script. You can set this value with `&chdir`. Scripts can get the current directory with `&cwd`. All file operations take this value into account.

```
chdir("/etc");
println(cwd());

$handle = openf("passwd");
```

/etc

Query the directory structure of the file system with the `&ls` and `&listRoots` functions. Use `&mkdir` to create new directories.

```
# a functional way to recurse all files.

map({
   if (-isDir $1)
```

```
    {
        map($this, ls($1));
    }
    else
    {
        println($1);
    }
}, listRoots());
```

/.DS_Store
/.hotfiles.btree
/Applications/.DS_Store
/Applications/.localized
/Applications/Address Book.app/Contents/Info.plist
...

Get a file size with `&lof` which stands for length of file. Rename files with `&rename` or do away with them using `&deleteFile`.

`&getFileName`, `&getFileParent`, and `&getFileProper` are available to parse and create filenames in a platform neutral way.

```
$path = getFileProper("/Users/raffi/", "fizz", "buzz/", "foo.txt");
println($path);
```

/Users/raffi/fizz/buzz/foo.txt

Example: Working with Large Datasets

Ever had to write a script that processes so much data that it eventually runs out of memory? Is your name Marty? If you answered yes to either of these questions then read this secton. Working with large data sets sometimes requires swapping data to the disk and reconstituting it.

This example uses an access ordered hash as a least-recently-used cache for data stored on the file system. The cache flushes the least recently used data to the disk as it grows in size. The cache restores flushed data when it is requested in the future.

```
debug(7);

# if a miss occurs, check if the key is cached
# in the current directory and load it.
sub missPolicy
{
    local('$handle $data');

    if (-exists $2)
```

```
   {
      $handle = openf($2);
      $data = readObject($handle);
      closef($handle);

      println("--- Loaded $2");
      return $data;
   }

   return $null;
}

# if the size of the data structure is over 3
# elements then save it to the disk.
sub removalPolicy
{
   local('$handle');

   if (size($1) >= 3)
   {
      $handle = openf("> $+ $2");
      writeObject($handle, $3);
      closef($handle);

      println("+++ Saved $2");
      return 1;
   }

   return 0;
}

# lets test it out...
global('%data');

%data = ohasha();
setMissPolicy(%data, &missPolicy);
setRemovalPolicy(%data, &removalPolicy);

add(%data, a => "apple", b => "batz", c => "cats");
println(%data);

println("Access 'a': " . %data["a"]);
println(%data);

add(%data, d => "dog");
println(%data);

println("Access 'b': " . %data["b"]);
println(%data);
```

$ **java -jar sleep.jar cache.sl**
%(a => 'apple', b => 'batz', c => 'cats')
Access 'a': apple
%(b => 'batz', c => 'cats', a => 'apple')
+++ Saved b
%(c => 'cats', a => 'apple', d => 'dog')
--- Loaded b
+++ Saved c
Access 'b': batz
%(a => 'apple', d => 'dog', b => 'batz')

This example serializes Sleep data with `&readObject` and `&writeObject`. These functions can convert most Sleep data to bytes and dump them to a stream.

As a side note: serialization is sensitive to the version of Sleep and Java you are using. Objects written using Java 1.5 and Sleep 2.1 can be written to and read from eachother. Objects written using Sleep running on top of Java 1.6 may not be compatible with Sleep running on top of Java 1.5.

Console

Most applications have access to a STDIN and STDOUT file to read and write data to the operator console. Sleep is no different. Sleep's I/O functions default to the console when no *$handle* is specified.

```
print("What is your name? ");

$name = readln();
println("Hello $name $+ , it is a pleasure to meet you.");
```

What is your name? **Raphael**
Hello Raphael, it is a pleasure to meet you.

Use `&getConsole` to obtain the *$handle* for the console.

Network Client/Server

Writing TCP/IP clients in Sleep is very easy. Simply use the `&connect` function to establish a connection to a server:

```
$handle = connect(@ARGV[0], 31337);

println($handle, "hello echo server");

$text = readln($handle);
println("Read: $text");
```

```
closef($handle);
```

$ **java -jar sleep.jar echocl.sl 127.0.0.1**
Read: PONG! hello echo server

The example above is a client for an echo service. The corresponding server for this echo client is:

```
$socket = listen(31337, 60 * 1000, $host);

println("Received connection from $host");

$text = readln($socket);
println("Read: $text");

println($socket, "PONG! $text");

closef($socket);
```

$ **java -jar sleep.jar echosrv.sl**
Received connection from 127.0.0.1
Read: hello echo server

The first call to `&listen` will register your script with the operating system as owning the specified network port. Subsequent calls to `&listen` accept a waiting connection attempt or block until a connection attempt occurs. To stop your application from listening on a port use `&closef` with the port number as a parameter.

To close the write portion of an I/O handle (causing a potential end-of-file on the other end) use `&printEOF`.

Use `-eof` to check if a connection is still open for reading.

Use `&fork` to write multithreaded servers. Polling is also possible. Use `&available` to check the number of bytes available on a handle.

```
$handle = connect("www.yahoo.com", 80);
println($handle, "GET /");
sleep(3000);

println(available($handle) . " bytes are available");
```

9562 bytes are available

Threads (Pipe I/O)

A thread is an asynchronous unit of execution. Threads in Sleep execute independent of eachother. They can be thought of as separate programs executing independent of one another. Threads do not share data by default. They can share data but then your responsibility as a programmer increases. Sleep threads can communicate with an I/O channel known as a pipe. These topics are covered in this section. First I'd like to go back to network clients and servers.

This example demonstrates a multithreaded echo server using `&fork` and `&listen`:

```
sub echoClient
{
   $text = readln($socket);
   println($socket, "back at ya: $text");
   closef($socket);
}

while (1)
{
   $server = listen(8888, 0);
   fork(&echoClient, $socket => $server);
}
```

$ **telnet 127.0.0.1 8888**
Connected to localhost.
hello world
back at ya: hello world
Connection closed by foreign host.
$ **telnet 127.0.0.1 8888**
Connected to localhost.
uNF
back at ya: uNF
Connection closed by foreign host.

This example uses a while loop to listen for and accept connections. Each connection receives its own thread.

Sharing Data

`&fork` accepts any number of key value pairs to share data between the current thread and the new thread. Pass by value and pass by reference rules apply to `&fork` arguments. If you want to share an updateable value between threads store it in a shared hash or array.

Code that manipulates shared data in a thread is known as a critical section. Semaphores exist to protect critical sections of code. Semaphores are flexible locks with atomic `&acquire` and `&release` operations.

Sleep associates a count with each semaphore. This count determines the number of threads that can `&acquire` the semaphore before a `&release`. A semaphore with a count of 1 is a binary semaphore. A binary semaphore allows only one thread to `&acquire` it before a `&release`.

This example uses a binary semaphore as a lock to protect a shared resource.

```
sub computation
{
   for ($x = 0; $x < 50000; $x++)
   {
      acquire($lock);
      %share["resource"] += $number;
      release($lock);
   }
}

%share["resource"] = 0;
$lock = semaphore(1);

$a = fork(&computation, \%share, \$lock, $number => 1);
$b = fork(&computation, \%share, \$lock, $number => -1);

wait($a); wait($b);
println(%share["resource"]);
```

```
0
```

In this example one thread increments and another decrements a shared resource. The protection must work as the end result is zero. Does this protection really matter? I can understand some skepticism. Here is the same example without the protection:

```
sub computation
{
   for ($x = 0; $x < 50000; $x++)
   {
      %share["resource"] += $number;
   }
}

%share["resource"] = 0;

$a = fork(&computation, \%share, $number => 1);
$b = fork(&computation, \%share, $number => -1);
```

```
wait($a); wait($b);
println(%share["resource"]);
```

```
2523
```

Not the expected value is it? The end lesson: protect your shared resources with semaphores!

Inter-thread communication

Like other I/O functions, `&fork` returns an I/O handle when called. Scripts can write to and read from this handle. But what are they reading from or writing to? `&fork` creates a global variable *$source* within each thread. This variable is the other end of the pipe returned by `&fork`. Data written to *$source* is read from the fork handle. Data written to the fork handle is read at *$source*.

Scripts can use this pipe for inter-thread communication.

```
sub a
{
   println("This is thread a");

   while $value (readln($source))
   {
      println("Read: $value");
   }

   println("done!");
}

$handle = fork(&a);
println($handle, "hello a");
println($handle, "blah blah");
closef($handle);
```

```
This is thread a
Read: hello a
Read: blah blah
done!
```

Sometimes it is helpful to communicate values between threads. Scripts can only communicate copies as the threads are isolated from eachother. Use `&readObject` and `&writeObject` to copy values between threads.

```
sub a
{
```

```
   @data = @("a", "b", "c");
   writeObject($source, @data);

   @stuff = @(1, 2, 3);
   writeObject($source, @stuff);
}

$handle = fork(&a);

@a = readObject($handle);
println("Read array: " . @a);

@b = readObject($handle);
println("Read array: " . @b);
```

```
Read array: @('a', 'b', 'c')
Read array: @(1, 2, 3)
```

Connecting two I/O connections

`&fork` can connect two I/O handles together into a virtual pipe. This example implements a generic TCP/IP client with this technique:

```
debug(7);
global('$host $port $socket');

sub handler
{
   local('$text');

   while $text (readln($src))
   {
      println($dst, $text);
   }

   closef($dst);
}

# obtain our host, port from the command line arguments
($host, $port) = @ARGV;

# connect to the desired host:port combination
$socket = connect($host, $port);

# fork the reader for the socket; prints all output to the console
fork(&handler, $src => $socket, $dst => getConsole());
```

```
# fork the reader for the console; prints all output to the socket
fork(&handler, $src => getConsole(), $dst => $socket);
```

$ **java -jar connect.sl irc.blessed.net 6667**
USER a b c :the phanton menace
NICK rawClient
PING :F826A790
PONG :F826A790
:irc.blessed.net 001 rawClient :Welcome to the EFNet Internet Relay Chat Network rawClient
JOIN #jircii
:rawClient!~a@cpe-72-226-177-132.twcny.res.rr.com JOIN :#jircii
:irc.blessed.net 332 rawClient #jircii :http://jircii.hick.org b42 (11.26.07) released! | http://blog.printf.no | sign up for the sleep google group: http://sleep.hick.org/
:irc.blessed.net 353 rawClient = #jircii :rawClient ceelow Drakx_ ph @Drakx[L] @Drakx @[Serge] @strider_ @seph_ @ph__ @ph____ @iHTC @`butane
:irc.blessed.net 366 rawClient #jircii :End of /NAMES list.
PRIVMSG #jircii :hi
QUIT :good bye!
:rawClient!~a@cpe-72-226-177-132.twcny.res.rr.com QUIT :Client Quit
ERROR :Closing Link: cpe-72-226-177-132.twcny.res.rr.com (Client Quit)

Waiting for a thread to complete

Sometimes it is helpful to spin off a new thread of execution, do some stuff in the current thread, and then wait for the new thread to complete. This is a join operation. Use `&wait` to join two threads. The `&wait` function will block until the thread completes or *$source* is closed.

```
sub factorial
{
   sub calculateFactorial
   {
      return iff($1 == 0, 1, $1 * calculateFactorial($1 - 1));
   }

   $result = calculateFactorial($value);
   println("fact( $+ $value $+ ) is ready");
   return $result;
}

$fact12 = fork(&factorial, $value => 120.0);
$fact11 = fork(&factorial, $value => 110.0);
$fact10 = fork(&factorial, $value => 100.0);

println("fact(120) = " . wait($fact12));
```

```
println("fact(110) = " . wait($fact11));
println("fact(100) = " . wait($fact10));
```

fact(120.0) is ready
fact(110.0) is ready
fact(100.0) is ready
fact(120) = 6.689502913449124E198
fact(110) = 1.5882455415227421E178
fact(100) = 9.33262154439441E157

External Programs

Interacting with an external program is very similar to interacting with a thread. The `&exec` function returns a handle that acts as a pipe between Sleep and an external program. This pipe provides access to the program's standard input (STDIN) and standard output (STDOUT).

```
$handle = exec("./printargs apple boy charlie");
printAll(readAll($handle));
closef($handle);
```

Arg 0 is: ./printargs
Arg 1 is: apple
Arg 2 is: boy
Arg 3 is: charlie

`&exec` accepts a command in two forms. The first form is a simple string. If a string is provided, Sleep will tokenize the string using whitespace as the delimeter. `&exec` uses the first token as the command and the subsequent tokens as individual arguments.

`&exec` also accepts an array instead of a string. The first element of the array is the command. The other elements represent the arguments. These arguments may contain whitespace or any other special characters.

```
$handle = exec(@("./printargs", "Hello world", "I have spaces"));
printAll(readAll($handle));
closef($handle);
```

Arg 0 is: ./printargs
Arg 1 is: Hello world
Arg 2 is: I have spaces

To kill a process use `&closef` on the *$handle*.

`&wait` on a process *$handle* will return the exit value of the process.

STDERR (and other manipulations of IOObject)

STDERR is the standard error stream. Sleep does not provide a function for obtaining a handle to STDERR. This is not an issue because you can get a handle for STDERR with a few object expressions.

Sleep's I/O library is an abstraction built on top of Java's `java.io.InputStream` and `java.io.OutputStream` classes.

Most handles have a source associated with them. Use the `getSource` method of `IOObject` to obtain the source backing the handle.

```
$handle = openf("a.txt");
$source = [$handle getSource];
$class  = [$source getClass];

println("Source of \$handle is $class");
```

Source of $handle is class java.io.File

The `&exec` handle is backed by a `java.lang.Process`. The `Process` class convienently provides a `getErrorStream` method. `getErrorStream` returns an `InputStream`.

Scripts can fuse an arbitrary `InputStream` or `OutputStream` into an I/O handle. Do this with the `getIOHandle` method in the `sleep.runtime.SleepUtils` class. This next example illustrates this technique.

```
$handle = exec("./printargs");

sub processStderr
{
   $source = [$handle getSource];      # java.lang.Process
   $stream = [$source getErrorStream]; # java.io.InputStream

   $stderr = [SleepUtils getIOHandle: $stream, $null];

   while $error (readln($stderr))
   {
      println("[stderr] $error");
   }
}

# process stderr in a new thread
fork(&processStderr, \$handle);

printAll(readAll($handle));
```

[stderr] No additional arguments specified.
Arg 0 is: ./printargs

The `getIOHandle` method in `SleepUtils` expects an `InputStream` and `OutputStream` argument. This example uses *$null* for the `OutputStream` to create a read-only handle.

Backtick Expressions

Scripts can execute a process with a string enclosed in backticks. The interpreter evaluates a backtick as a parsed literal and then executes the resulting string. The output of the execution is returned as an array.

```
# recursively find all files
@files = `find .`;

# print out the number of files we found
println("There are " . size(@files) . " files here. :)");
```

There are 2948 files here. :)

Scripts can retrieve execution errors through `&checkError`.

Buffers

For times when speed is a necessity Sleep provides the friendly byte buffer. A buffer is a segment of memory that scripts can write to (and eventually read from) using Sleep's I/O functions. Buffers are fast. If there is a need to concatenate lots of data or to manipulate streams of data then buffers are a must.

To allocate a buffer use the `&allocate` function. Buffers are write-only once allocated.

```
$buffer = allocate(1024 * 10); # allocate a 10K buffer
```

Scripts can write to a buffer just like a file:

```
println($buffer, "this is some text, in the buff!");
writeb($buffer, 33);
```

`&closef` on a write-only buffer will make the contents available for reading. Consequently the buffer is read-only from this point.

```
closef($buffer);
$string = readln($buffer);
$byte   = readb($buffer, 1);
```

Calling `&closef` on a read-only buffer will deallocate the buffer's resources.

The following program encrypts a file using a simple XOR encryption scheme. It uses the allocated buffer as a convienent place to hold data before dumping it to a file.

```
# read the file in
$input = openf(@ARGV[0]);
$data = readb($input, -1);
closef($input);

# encrypt the contents of the file...
$buffer = allocate(strlen($data));

for ($x = 0; $x < strlen($data); $x++)
{
   writeb($buffer, chr(byteAt($data, $x) ^ 0x34));
}

closef($buffer); # buffer is readable now..
$data = readb($buffer, strlen($data));

# write the file out
$output = openf(">" . @ARGV[0]);
writeb($output, $data);
closef($output);
```

$ **cat >contents.txt**
pHEAR the reapz0r
$ **java -jar sleep.jar encryptxor.sl contents.txt**
$ **cat contents.txt**
D|quf@\QFQUDNF>
$ **java -jar sleep.jar encryptxor.sl contents.txt**
$ **cat contents.txt**
pHEAR the reapz0r

8.2 String I/O

An important distinction between String I/O and Binary I/O is the interpretation of the data. Sleep's string I/O functions are unicode aware.

Many programmers are comfortable with ASCII. ASCII is a common agreement on what characters are represented by the integers 0-127. Most times an ASCII character is stored in 8-bits. This leaves 128-255 open for interpretation. Different "character sets" evolved over time. Some character sets used these high-ascii characters to represent accented characters for other languages. My favorite, Cp437, used them to represent line drawing characters in a terminal.

This use of ASCII as a string representation has some limitations. For example, applications are limited to 128 extra characters. This is not enough for some languages. The other problem is a lack of a way to identify which character set is in use.

To solve these problems unicode was invented. Unicode is a standard universal mapping for all known characters you would ever care to represent on a screen.

Java uses UTF-16 to store unicode characters in memory. This means each character is represented with 2 bytes. `&readc` consumes 2-bytes from a handle to read a UTF-16 character. Other functions such as `&print`, `&println`, `&readln`, etc. read and write 1 byte ASCII characters. These functions rely on a character set encoding to remap the extended characters.

Your platform has a default encoding associated with it. For the most part this is transparent to you and you'll never care about the distinction. You can use `&setEncoding` to specify which encoding to use when reading from or writing to a handle.

`&pack`, `&unpack`, `&bwrite`, and `&bread` can read and write strings of 16-bit characters. The size difference between encoded characters and UTF-16 is demonstrated below:

```
# encoded output

$handle_a = openf(">a.txt");
println($handle_a, "apple");
closef($handle_a);

println("Encoded output: " . lof("a.txt") . " bytes");

# UTF-16 output

$handle_b = openf(">b.txt");
bwrite($handle_b, "u", "apple");
closef($handle_b);

println("UTF-16  output: " . lof("b.txt") . " bytes");
```

```
Encoded output: 6 bytes
UTF-16  output: 12 bytes
```

Joel Spolsky's weblog has a great introduction to unicode and the concepts discussed here: http://www.joelonsoftware.com/articles/Unicode.html

8.3 Binary I/O

Scripts can read and write bytes with &readb and &writeb. Sleep stores sequences of bytes in string scalars. This means you can use &substr, &strlen, and other string manipulation functions on binary data. Use &byteAt to get a byte from a string.

```
# simple file copy program.
# java -jar sleep.jar copy.sl <target> <destination>

($target_f, $dest_f) = @ARGV;

$handle = openf($target_f);
$data = readb($handle, -1);
closef($handle);

$handle = openf("> $+ $dest_f);
writeb($handle, $data);
closef($handle);
```

This example is a file copy script. Nothing too special here. This script opens a file, reads all of its contents in, and writes them out.

Interpreting Bytes

Computers store all data as 1s and 0s at some point. Since computers store all data this way, it makes sense that any data can be interpreted in different ways.

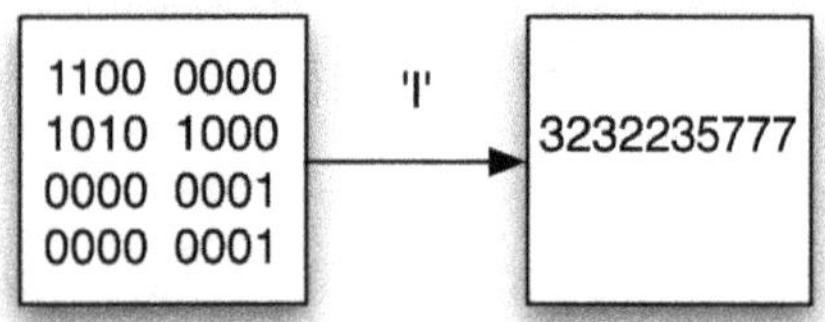

Above we have a 32 bit string of 1s and 0s. When interpreted as an integer this string has the value 3,232,235,777. Let us interpret this same string as 4 separate bytes:

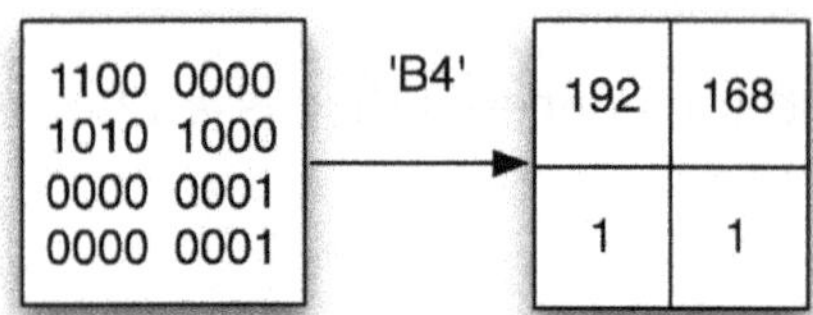

This is the same 32bit string. Each byte contains 8 bits so the whole string yields 4 bytes. The value of each is 192, 168, 1, and 1.

```
$ java -jar sleep.jar
>> Welcome to the Sleep scripting language
> interact
>> Welcome to interactive mode.
Type your code and then '.' on a line by itself to execute the code.
Type Ctrl+D or 'done' on a line by itself to leave interactive mode.
$bytes = pack("I", 3232235777L);
@bytes = unpack("B4", $bytes);
println(@bytes);
.
@(192, 168, 1, 1)
println(formatNumber( 3232235777L, 10, 2));
.
11000000101010000000000100000001
```

Pack and Unpack

`&pack` and `&unpack` condense and extract Sleep types to and from byte strings. These functions interpret data as specified in a template.

`&pack` accepts a template and a comma separated list of items to pack into a byte string. `&unpack` accepts a byte string and extracts items according to the template.

The template characters:

Character	Bytes	Description
b	1	byte (-128 to 127) (converted to/from a sleep int)
B	1	unsigned byte (0 to 255) (converted to/from a sleep int)
c	2	UTF-16 Unicode character
C	1	normal character
d	8	double (uses IEEE 754 floating-point "double format" bit layout)
f	4	float (uses IEEE 754 floating-point "single format" bit layout)
h	1	a hex byte (low nybble first)
H	1	a hex byte (high nybble first)
i	4	integer
I	4	unsigned integer (converted to/from a sleep long)
l	8	long
M	0	mark this point in the IO stream (for reads only)
o	variable	sleep scalar object (used to serialize/deserialize scalars)

Character	Bytes	Description
R	0	reset this stream to the last mark point (reads only)
s	2	short (converted to/from a sleep int)
S	2	unsigned short (converted to/from a sleep int)
u	variable	read/write UTF-16 character data until terminated with a null byte. (see note below)
U	variable	read/write the specified number of UTF-16 characters (consumes the whole field)
x	1	skips a byte/writes a nully byte in/to this stream (no data returned)
z	variable	read/write character data until terminated with a null byte. (see note below)
Z	variable	read/write the specified number of characters (consumes the whole field)

Follow up any of the template characters with an integer to repeat that element some number of times. Use a `*` to indicate that all remaining data should be interpreted with the most recent character. Whitespace is ignored inside of template strings.

Network byte (big endian) order is the default for all reads/writes. Scripts can indicate endianess if they choose. A + appended to a template character indicates big endian. A - appended to a character indicates little endian. The `!` indicates the platform native byte order.

This example discovers the native byte order of your CPU:

```
$endianess = iff(unpack('i!', pack('i+', 1))[0] == 1, "big", "little");
```

I'm on a mac:

```
$ java -jar sleep.jar
>> Welcome to the Sleep scripting language
> x iff(unpack('i!', pack('i+', 1))[0] == 1, "big endian", "little endian")
big endian
$ uname -a
Darwin beardsley.local 8.8.0 Darwin Kernel Version 8.8.0: Fri Sep  8 17:18:57 PDT 2006;
root:xnu-792.12.6.obj~1/RELEASE_PPC Power Macintosh powerpc
```

Interoperability with C

One powerful feature of pack and unpack is interoperability with C. Think of a pack and unpack template as the definition of a C struct. Each template character represents a member of the struct.

This C program creates two records and serializes them to a file (and you thought this was a Sleep/Java book):

```
#include <stdio.h>
#include <string.h>
#include <time.h>

struct record
{
   char name[16];
   int  age;
   long created;
};

int main(int argc, char * argv[])
{
   FILE * file = fopen("records.bin", "wb");

   if (file != NULL)
   {
      struct record data;

      /* populate our data structure with some bogus data */
      strcpy(data.name, "Raphael");
      data.age     = 26;
      data.created = time(NULL);

      fwrite(&data, sizeof data, 1, file);

      /* populate our data structure with more bogus data */
      strcpy(data.name, "Frances");
      data.age     = 25;
      data.created = time(NULL);

      fwrite(&data, sizeof(struct record), 1, file);

      fclose(file);
   }
}
```

For my next magic trick, I will use Sleep to extract this information and display it right before your very eyes.

To prove I'm not cheating:

$ **gcc interop.c -o interop**
$ **./interop**
$ **hexdump -C records.bin**

```
00000000  52 61 70 68 61 65 6c 00  00 00 00 00 8f e0 71 84  |Raphael.......q.|
00000010  00 00 00 1a 46 75 f6 e9  46 72 61 6e 63 65 73 00  |....Fu..Frances.|
00000020  00 00 00 00 8f e0 71 84  00 00 00 19 46 75 f6 e9  |......q.....Fu..|
00000030
$ date
Sun Jun 17 23:08:58 EDT 2007
```

The first step is to create a template that represents the following C structure.

```
struct record
{
   char name[16];
   int  age;
   long created;
}
```

This structure contains a 30 character string, an int field, and a date value stored as a long.

The template to unpack this data is: `'Z30 i I'`.

The code to parse the records file above is:

```
$handle = openf("records.bin");

while @data (bread($handle, 'Z16 i I'))
{
   ($name, $age, $created) = @data;
   $created = formatDate($created * 1000, 'EEE, d MMM yyyy HH:mm:ss Z');
   println("Name: $name $+ \nAge: $age $+ \nCreated: $created");
}

closef($handle);
```

This script uses `&bread` to read each struct entry into an array. This script multiplies the extracted time by 1000 to convert it to milliseconds. Sleep represents date time values in milliseconds.

And here is the output of the extractor script:

```
$ java -jar sleep.jar interop.sl
Name: Raphael
Age: 26
Created: Sun, 17 Jun 2007 23:07:21 -0400
Name: Frances
Age: 25
Created: Sun, 17 Jun 2007 23:07:21 -0400
```

9. Sleep Integration

9.1 Embed Sleep

This chapter is a different spin from the rest of the manual. Here I will show practices and conventions to embed and extend Sleep for your purposes. I will also cover how to manipulate data. Reading through this chapter will get you started with Sleep integration. To go further read through the Sleep API Javadoc at http://sleep.dashnine.org/docs/api/.

Integration Basics

The first integration task is loading a script and catching syntax errors.

```
import sleep.runtime.ScriptInstance;
import sleep.runtime.ScriptLoader;
import sleep.error.YourCodeSucksException;

...

ScriptLoader loader = new ScriptLoader();

try
{
   ScriptInstance script = loader.loadScript("script.sl");
}
catch (YourCodeSucksException syntaxErrors)
```

```
{
   System.out.println(syntaxErrors.formatErrors());
}
catch (IOException ioError)
{
   ...
}
```

This code instantiates a `sleep.runtime.ScriptLoader`. This class manages a lot of details for loading scripts and installing extensions. You should use it even if your application has one script.

When a script is loaded it is first read in from a file or a stream. The textual representation of the script is then compiled into a `sleep.engine.Block`. Naturally there is some overhead to compile a script into a `Block`. To skip this overhead you can use the `compileScript` method of `ScriptLoader`.

Optionally, the `ScriptLoader` can cache scripts for you. To enable this feature call the `setGlobalCache` method.

Sleep only throws exceptions at compile time. Runtime script errors are caught through a `sleep.error.RuntimeWarningWatcher` interface. The purpose of this mechanism is to allow you to intercept errors and notify the user of them.

```
import sleep.error.RuntimeWarningWatcher;
import sleep.error.ScriptWarning;

public class Watchdog implements RuntimeWarningWatcher
{
   public void processScriptWarning(ScriptWarning warning)
   {
       System.out.println(warning);
   }
}
```

To catch errors, you must install a `RuntimeWarningWatcher` into a `sleep.runtime.ScriptInstance`.

```
script.addWarningWatcher(new Watchdog());
```

Debug and trace messages are also passed through the `RuntimeWarningWatcher` mechanism. Use the `isDebugTrace` method from `sleep.error.ScriptWarning` to query if the message is a trace or not.

The last step is to execute the script itself.

```
script.runScript()
```

Automatic Setup on Load

As we move through this chapter you will notice there is an abundance of stuff to do everytime a script is loaded. To help manage this Sleep includes a mechanism called `sleep.interfaces.Loadable` bridges. Bridges are extensions to the Sleep language. A `Loadable` bridge is called every time a script is loaded and unloaded. You may associate any number of `Loadable` bridges with a `ScriptLoader` instance.

This `Loadable` bridge assigns the Watchdog `RuntimeWarningWatcher` to every new `ScriptInstance`:

```
import sleep.interfaces.Loadable;
import sleep.runtime.ScriptInstance;

public class ThingsToDo implements Loadable
{
   public void scriptLoaded(ScriptInstance script)
   {
      script.addWarningWatcher(new Watchdog());
```

`Loadable` bridges do nothing without the `ScriptLoader`. There are two ways to install this type of bridge. A `Loadable` extension installed as a specific bridge is executed for every script load and unload, no matter what. Use a specific bridge when a task has to be done for every script. Adding a `RuntimeWarningWatcher` is an example of such a task.

```
ScriptLoader loader = new ScriptLoader();
loader.addSpecificBridge(new ThingsTodDo());
```

A global bridge is installed once for each script environment. Sharing of a script environment is discussed in a later section. The purpose of a global bridge is to populate a script environment with functions, operators, and predicates. Global bridges save the `ScriptLoader` from unnecessary work.

Add global bridges with the `addGlobalBridge` method of `ScriptLoader`.

Put and Get Scalars

Use the `putScalar` method of `sleep.runtime.ScriptVariables` to set a value in a script.

```
ScriptVariables variables = script.getScriptVariables();
variables.putScalar("$foo", SleepUtils.getScalar("foo!"));
```

To obtain a scalar from a script:

```
Scalar value = variables.getScalar("$foo");
System.out.println(value.toString());
```

Variable Containers

The ScriptVariables object mantains variables and scope information for a script instance. Each scope is its own container of scalars. Sleep holds a scope in an object that implements the sleep.interfaces.Variable interface. You can implement the Variable interface and alter how scalars are stored and accessed.

It is possible to implement the Variable interface and alter how scalars are stored and accessed. This next example installs a hypothetical MyVariable implementation into a script.

```
ScriptVariables variableManager = new ScriptVariables(new MyVariable());
script.setScriptVariables(variableManager);
```

The Sleep Console

The sleep console is an interactive console for working with sleep scripts. The console includes commands for loading scripts, running scripts, and dumping an abstract syntax tree of parsed scripts. Integrating the sleep console consists of building a console proxy that provides input/output services for the actual Sleep Console.

An example console proxy (using STDIN/STDOUT) is below:

```
import sleep.io.*;
import sleep.console.ConsoleProxy;

public class MyConsoleProxy implements ConsoleProxy
{
   protected BufferedRead in;

   public MyConsoleProxy()
   {
      in = new BufferedReader(new InputStreamReader(System.in));
   }

   public void consolePrint(String message)
   {
      System.out.print(message);
   }

   public void consolePrintln(Object message)
   {
      System.out.println(message.toString());
```

```
    }

    public String consoleReadln()
    {
        try
        {
            return in.readLine();
        }
        catch (IOException ex)
        {
            ex.printStackTrace();
            return null;
        }
    }
}
```

To instantiate the Sleep Console and install a custom console proxy:

```
import sleep.runtime.ScriptEnvironment;

ConsoleImplementation console = new ConsoleImplementation(environment,
variables, loader);

console.setProxy(new MyConsoleProxy());
console.rppl(); // starts the console
```

This code instantiates a sleep console with the specified function environment, script variables, and script loader. Once an implementation of the `sleep.console.ConsoleProxy` interface is installed the sleep console is ready to use. Any application taking advantage of the sleep console should :instantiate it before scripts are loaded. This is necessary as the sleep console installs itself as a `Loadable` bridge into the `ScriptLoader`.

Can I embed Sleep with JSR 223, the javax.script API?

Java 1.6 includes a new programming interface (the javax.script API) to allow interchangeable use of different script engines. Sleep 2.1 supports this interface.

To obtain the Sleep script engine factory:

```
import javax.script.ScriptEngineManager;
import javax.script.ScriptEngine;
import javax.script.ScriptException;
```

```
...

ScriptEngineManager manager = new ScriptEngineManager();
ScriptEngine sleepEngine = manager.getEngineByName("sleep");
```

To evaluate a script:

```
try
{
   sleepEngine.eval("println('hello world!');");
}
catch (ScriptException exception)
{
   /* syntax errors are wrapped in a ScriptException object */
   System.out.println(exception.getMessage());
}
```

The javax.script API supports the concept of "bindings" to act as shared variables between scripts. A binding named 'frame' containing a `JFrame` object is available as a variable named *$frame* that contains a sleep object scalar with the `JFrame` object.

The `ScriptContext.GLOBAL_SCOPE` bindings are installed as global variables. The `ScriptContext.ENGINE_SCOPE` bindings are available as local variables.

The javax.script API also has a ScriptContext object for specifying where to dump errors, receive input strings, and write output strings. My experiments honoring the values of this object with jrunscript were less than happy. As such Sleep ignores these values and dumps everything to `System.in` and `System.out`.

For more information see the javax.script API documentation: http://java.sun.com/javase/6/docs/api/javax/script/package-summary.html

9.2 Manage Multiple Scripts

Sleep was built to manage multiple scripts operating within a single application. When managing multiple scripts there are issues surrounding multi-threading and allowing scripts to share functions and data. Of course you get to choose how much sharing should occur. Scripts can either execute completely isolated of eachother or they can share everything including variables.

Sharing Functions and Bridges

Every script has an environment associated with it. The environment is a `java.util.Hashtable` object associated with the `sleep.runtime.ScriptEnvironment` class. This `Hashtable` object contains all of the bridges (functions, operators) available to your Sleep scripts. Every time a script is loaded the environment is populated with the default bridges and any bridges that you elect to install through a `Loadable` interface. There is some overhead constructing this environment for each script. Bridge objects are not supposed to save state so it is generally safe to share the environment `Hashtable` object amongst scripts. This will enable all scripts to share functions and bridges amongst eachother.

The `ScriptLoader` class has several versions of the `loadScript` method that accept a `Hashtable` environment as a parameter.

```
import java.util.Hashtable;
import sleep.runtime.ScriptLoader;
import sleep.runtime.ScriptInstance;

...

Hashtable environment = new Hashtable();
ScriptLoader loader = new ScriptLoader();

try
{
   ScriptInstance a = loader.loadScript("script1.sl", environment);

   ...

   ScriptInstance b = loader.loadScript("script2.sl", environment);
```

There is some potential for data leakage amongst multiple scripts. Sleep closures (every subroutine is created as a closure) maintain state within themselves. This includes their closure scope variables and their continuation data (in the event of callcc, yield, etc.). Take this into consideration when choosing to share environments.

Sharing Script Variables

Script variables are managed by a `ScriptVariables` instance held by the `ScriptInstance` object. You can obtain this object with the `getScriptVariables` method and you are free to set it with the `setScriptVariables` method.

This example shows how to share variables amongst two scripts.

```
import sleep.runtime.ScriptVariables
import sleep.runtime.ScriptLoader
import sleep.runtime.ScriptInstance

...

ScriptVariables variables = new ScriptVariables();

try
{
   ScriptInstance a = loader.loadScript("script1.sl", environment);
   a.setScriptVariables(variables);

   ...

   ScriptInstance b = loader.loadScript("script2.sl", environment);
   b.setScriptVariables(variables);
```

In my oppinion it makes no sense to share script variables without also sharing the environment.

Multithreading

Sleep scripts happily work in a multi-threaded application. This is accomplished by internal synchronization that allows only one function to execute at any given time. As soon as a function begins it must complete before another Sleep function in another thread may execute. Sleep internally synchronizes on the `ScriptVariables` object held by each `ScriptInstance`.

Functions such as `&fork` work by creating an isolated clone of the current `ScriptInstance`. This is accomplished through the `fork` method of `ScriptInstance`. Forked code can run in multiple threads without blocking. This is because it shares as little as possible with its parent script. `&fork` creates an `sleep.bridges.io.IOObject` that acts as a handle for the thread. After initialization the `setThread` method is called to associate the child thread with the `IOObject`. The thread can pass a return value for the thread (obtained with `&wait`) with the `setToken` method.

9.3 Extend Sleep

Earlier we discussed an environment `Hashtable` object that stores operators, functions, etc. Operations, functions, predicates, and certain constructs are added to the language after the script is parsed. These are called bridges. The interpreter is flexible enough to look for them in the environment and send a request to them. Bridges are a powerful means for introducing new abstractions and functionality into the Sleep language.

Before extending Sleep it is worth asking yourself if you really have to? As discussed in chapter 7, Sleep is capable of accessing anything from the Java class library. Bridges have the benefit of being faster due to the lack of reflection overhead and you can design an interface that is appropriate for Sleep.

Function Bridge

The simplest bridge is the `sleep.interfaces.Function` bridge. This bridge adds one or more new functions to the Sleep language.

```
public class FooFunction implements Function
{
   public Scalar evaluate(String name, ScriptInstance script, Stack args)
   {
      System.out.println("function foo has been called");
      return SleepUtils.getEmptyScalar();
   }
}
```

Install this `Function` into the environment to make it available to scripts.

```
void scriptLoaded(ScriptInstance script)
{
   Hashtable env = script.getScriptEnvironment().getEnvironment();
   env.put("&foo", new FooFunction());
```

Notice that we begin the `foo` function with an ampersand. All functions begin with an ampersand. Now that `&foo` is installed it can be called as `foo()` within a script.

The evaluate method is expected to return a `sleep.runtime.Scalar` object. A `Scalar` is the universal container for Sleep data. Never return `null` directly. To return a null scalar use the `getEmptyScalar` method of `sleep.runtime.SleepUtils`.

To work with arguments passed to a built-in function:

```
public class MyAddFunction implements Function
{
   public Scalar evaluate(String name, ScriptInstance script, Stack args)
   {
      int arg1 = BridgeUtilities.getInt(args, 0);
      int arg2 = BridgeUtilities.getInt(args, 0);

      return SleepUtils.getScalar(arg1 + arg2);
   }
}
```

This function takes two arguments. The arguments are passed in as a `java.util.Stack` object. The `sleep.bridges.BridgeUtilities` class contains methods for safely extracting parameters from the arguments stack. In this example two integer parameters are extracted. The `BridgeUtilities` class allows a default value to be specified in case the stack is empty (i.e. not enough parameters were passed).

The last part of the above function is the return statement. Notice that the result of adding arg1 and arg2 is passed to `getScalar(int)` in `SleepUtils`. The `SleepUtils` class contains static methods for converting just about any type you can think of into a `Scalar` usable by sleep scripts.

Predicate and Operator Bridge

A predicate is an operator used inside of comparisons. Comparisons are used in if statements and loop constructs. `sleep.interfaces.Predicate` bridges are used to add new predicates to the language.

A binary predicate can have any name. A unary predicate always begins with the minus symbol. `isin` is a binary predicate and `-isletter` is a unary predicate.

An operator is anything used to operate on two variables inside of an expression. For example `2 + 3` is the expression to add `2` and `3`. The plus sign is the operator.

A predicate is created by implementing the interface `Predicate`. Likewise an operator is created by implementing the `sleep.interfaces.Operator` interface.

Register new predicates and operators with the `sleep.parser.ParserConfig` class before loading scripts.

```
ParserConfig.addKeyword("predicate");
```

The keyword registering practice is in place to clear up ambiguity when parsing scripts. The Sleep parser does not know what operators, functions, keywords it has. If you create an operator that follows the same naming rules as a function name, sleep might confuse left_hand_side operator (expression) for a function call. This is due to operator (expression) looking the same as function (expression) to the parser.

Environment Bridges

In the Sleep language a block of code associated with an identifier is processed by an `sleep.interfaces.Environment` bridge. Sleep implements the sub keyword with these. To declare a subroutine you use:

```
sub identifier { commands; }
```

The environment bridge associated with the keyword `sub` creates a new closure and saves it into the script environment as a function named `&identifier`.

In general a block of code is associated with an environment using the following syntax:

```
keyword identifier { commands; }
```

An environment bridge is created by implementing the `Environment` interface. An environment bridge should register its keyword with the script parser before any scripts are loaded. Sleep also offers two variations on the `Environment`.

The syntax for a `sleep.interfaces.FilterEnvironment` is:

```
keyword identifier "string" { commands; }
```

And the `sleep.interfaces.PredicateEnvironment`:

```
keyword (predicate) { commands; }
```

`Environment` bridges are great for implementing different paradigms.

Example: KeyBindingsBridge

I really started to appreciate Sleep when I used scripts to implement the menus and keyboard shortcuts in jIRCii. Hardcoding these things is a pain. Not to mention powerusers will want to change them anywyas. By making these items scriptable I reduced my overall development effort, gave users an example to script from, and I was able to eat my own dogfood with the scripting interface.

The jIRCii key bindings bridge uses an `Environment` installed with the keyword `bind`. This bridge lets users write scripts like this one:

```
bind Ctrl+D
{
   closeWindow(getActiveWindow());
}
```

The implementation has three components. The `Environment` bridge itself, the installation of the key dispatch listener, and the key dispatch listener.

```
/* A bridge that creates a bind keyword for use within Sleep scripts. */
public class KeyBindingsBridge implements KeyEventDispatcher,
                                          Environment, Loadable
{
   /** Storage for our bindings <String, Runnable> */
   protected Map bindings = new HashMap();
```

```
/** From the Environment interface */
public void bindFunction(ScriptInstance script, String typeKeyword,
                         String functionName, Block functionBody)
{
    SleepClosure runme = new SleepClosure(script, functionBody);
    bindings.put(functionName, runme);
}
```

This method is called whenever the `bind` keyword is encountered in a script. This method constructs a closure out of the code block and stores it into a `java.util.Map` for safe keeping. The key to the map is the actual keyboard shortcut to bind.

Of course Sleep can't use this `Environment` until you install it. This code installs this bridge into the `ScriptEnvironment`.

```
public void scriptLoaded(ScriptInstance script)
{
   script.getScriptEnvironment().getEnvironment().put("bind", this);
```

This code registers the KeyBindingsBridge as a global listener for key dispatches.

```
/* install this object as a listener for all key presses... don't worry
   only bound key events are swallowed.  Everything else passes through
   harmlessly */

   KeyboardFocusManager manager;
   manager = KeyboardFocusManager.getCurrentKeyboardFocusManager();
   manager.addKeyEventDispatcher(this);
```

This code responds to a key press.

```
/* called whenever a key is pressed. */
public boolean dispatchKeyEvent(KeyEvent ev)
{
    /* ignore non-key press events */

    if (ev.getID() != KeyEvent.KEY_PRESSED)
    {
        return false;
    }

    /* construct a description of the key press event */

    StringBuffer description = new StringBuffer();
    if (ev.getModifiers() != 0)
    {
       description.append(getKeyModifiers(ev));
```

```
        }

        description.append(getKeyText(ev));

        /* check if a script has bound this combination */

        if (bindings.containsKey(description.toString()))
        {
           /* grab the scripted handler from our bindings map */
           Runnable scriptedBind;
           scriptedBind = (Runnable)bindings.get(description.toString());

              // in case you're confused, SleepClosure implements the
              // Runnable interface.

           /* invoke the script in the event dispatcher thread */
           SwingUtilities.invokeLater(scriptedBind);

           /* consume the event */
           ev.consume();
           return true;
        }

        return false;
    }
```

And thats it. Whenever a key is pressed this method will check if the key combination is bound to a script. The script associated with the key combination is invoked. Any desktop app can immediately benefit from this type of extensibility.

Due to space constraints I am unable to include the entire source code for this example. To download it and play with it, visit:

- http://sleep.dashnine.org/download/keydemo.zip

The I/O Pipeline

No discussion of Sleep extension is complete without a discussion of the I/O pipeline. Sleep's I/O is built around `IOObject`. Each `IOObject` instance contains the read and write pipeline of a handle.

Sleep chains together multiple I/O streams to support its read, write, mark, and reset functions. This I/O chain is available from `IOObject` to implement your own I/O functions.

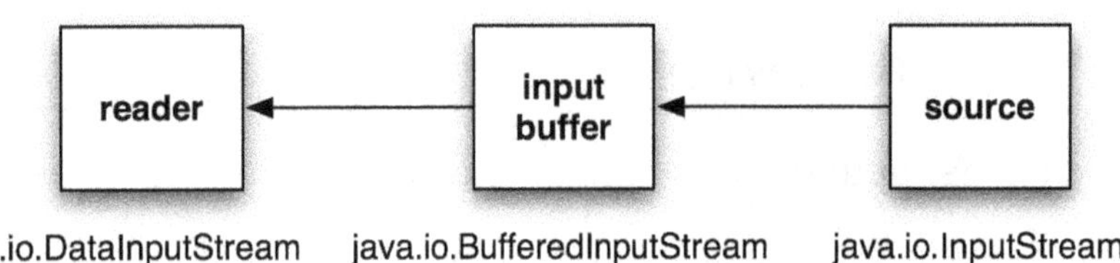

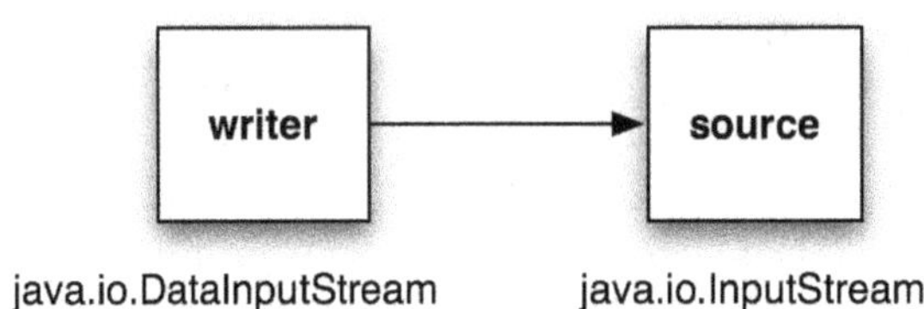

All Sleep handles are object scalars referencing an `IOObject` instance. To allow Sleep to interact with an I/O stream use the `openRead` and `openWrite` methods on a freshly instantiated `IOObject`.

```
public class FetchBridge implements Loadable, Function
{
   public void scriptLoaded(ScriptInstance script)
   {
       Hashtable env = script.getScriptEnvironment().getEnvironment();
       env.put("&fetch", this);
   }

   public Scalar evaluate(String name, ScriptInstance script, Stack args)
   {
       /* this function bridge implements a new I/O handle &fetch.
          &fetch accepts a URL and opens a stream for reading in the
          contents of the URL */

       URL address = new URL(BridgeUtilities.getString(args));

       IOObject temp = new IOObject();
       temp.openRead(address.openStream());
       return temp;
   }
```

Sleep refers to STDIN and STDOUT as the console. The console is specific to each script (regardless of shared environment). To obtain the console for a script use the `getConsole` method of `IOObject`. Likewise to set the console for a script use the `setConsole` method.

Store Bridge State

Sleep scripts share bridges and compiled scripts amongst eachother and sometimes across multiple threads. Sleep has a thread model that relies on isolation of script instances. To keep this isolation (while sharing where reasonable) make sure you don't store state in your scripts.

This is an example of where you can learn from my mistakes. The regular expression bridge used to store state to allow `&matched` to retrieve the results of the most recent `ismatch` and `hasmatch` comparisons. After I implemented `&fork` I started receiving complaints of very strange bugs in the regex engine. Eventually I figured out the problem. I created a content metadata mechanism to help solve it once and for all.

Sleep provides a context metadata mechanism for storing state. Context metadata is associated with the current closure scope. You can store and retrieve context objects using the `setContextMetadata("key", $object)` and `getContextMetadata("key")` methods in `ScriptEnvironment`.

This example demonstrates an accumulator function. The purpose of an accumulator is to store an integer and add 1 to it each time it is called. Naturally this accumulator function has to store some internal state. For this we use the context metadata mechanism:

```
public class Accumulator implements Function, Loadable
{
   public void scriptLoaded(ScriptInstance script)
   {
      script.getScriptEnvironment().getEnvironment().put("&accum", this);
   }

   public Scalar evaluate(String name, ScriptInstance script, Stack args)
   {
      ScriptEnvironment env = script.getScriptEnvironment();

      /* retrieve the accumulator value */
      Integer value = env.getContextMetadata("accum", new Integer(0));

      /* add one to the accumulator value */
      env.setContextMetadata("accum", new Integer(value.intValue() + 1));

      /* return the accumulated value (prior to accumulation) */
      return SleepUtils.getScalar(value.intValue());
```

Report Errors

Sleep makes a distinction between hard errors and soft errors. A hard error indicates a failure somewhere within Sleep (sometimes caused by the scripter!). Attempting to use a non-existent operator is an example of a hard error. A soft error is an error that can be recovered from. Attempting to access a non-existent file is a soft error.

Soft errors are accessible with the `&checkError` function or as a Sleep exception when debug mode 34 is enabled. Sleep accepts any type of object for soft errors.

```
public class FearFactor implements Function, Loadable
{
   public void scriptLoaded(ScriptInstance script)
   {
      script.getScriptEnvironment().put("&fear", this)
   }

   public Scalar evaluate(String name, ScriptInstance script, Stack args)
   {
      /* checkError($blah) will now return "fear me!" after calling this
         function */

      script.getScriptEnvironment().flagError("fear me!");
```

The best way to communicate a hard error is through a Java exception. This will allow Sleep to report the exception with the appropriate line number and script file. If a user failed to supply the correct arguments use an `java.lang.IllegalArgumentException`. Wrap everything else in a `java.lang.RuntimeException`.

```
public Scalar evaluate(String name, ScriptInstance script, Stack args)
{
   if (args.isEmpty())
   {
      throw new IllegalArgumentException(name + ": grrr!!!");
   }
```

The drawback to exceptions is they will cause the current function to exit with a *$null* return value. If you really want to display a warning use the `showDebugMessage` method of the `ScriptEnvironment` class.

```
public Scalar evaluate(String name, ScriptInstance script, Stack args)
{
   script.getScriptEnvironment().showDebugMessage("hello world!");
```

Warning: hello world! at script.sl:3

Taint Mode

To support security (and because I care), Sleep has a taint mode. Taint mode forces Sleep to taint variables received from external sources. This is a security mechanism to help educate scripters when they may be using tainted data within dangerous operations.

Terminology used here comes from the 'Run-time taint support proposal' [http://news.php.net/php.internals/26979] by Wietse Venema posted to the PHP internals mailing list.

Sleep's implementation of taint is designed to have no performance impact when turned off. When enabled taint mode wraps interpreter instructions with taint wrappers. These wrappers enforce the taint policy for an operation based on its category.

Wrapped instructions include operations and function calls. Parsed literals are treated as a special case.

Sleep has 4 taint value categories:

- **Sensitive functions** are not allowed to receive a tainted input. Any attempt to use tainted input with a sensitive function will result in a hard error. Sleep functions in this category are responsible for making themselves known. The mechanism for this is described below.
- **Permeable functions** return a tainted result only when their input is tainted. By default all Sleep functions fall into this category.
- **Tainter functions** always return tainted results. These functions are expected to self identify as well.
- **Sanitizer functions** always return an untainted value. These functions must self identify.

The taint mechanism depends on you to flag your Sleep extensions into the appropriate category. With this in mind Sleep tries to make this process as easy and transparent as possible.

```
public void scriptLoaded(ScriptInstance si)
{
   Hashtable env = si.getScriptEnvironment().getEnvironment();

   // install &foo as a Tainter function.
   env.put("&foo", TaintUtils.Tainter(this));

   // install &bar as a Sanitizer function.
   env.put("&bar", TaintUtils.Sanitizer(this));

   // install &dbquery as a Sensitive function.
   env.put("&dbquery", TaintUtils.Sensitive(this));
```

The `sleep.taint.TaintUtils` class contains static methods that accept different Sleep bridges as parameters. They return wrapped versions of these bridges if tainting is enabled. If tainting is disabled these functions merely return the original bridges that were passed in. If you're writing a bridge you merely need to identify which of your functions are sanitizers, tainters, or sensitive and wrap them as shown.

To set taint mode (globally):

```
/* do this before loading any scripts */
System.setProperty("sleep.taint", "true");
```

To check if taint mode is enabled use the `isTaintMode` method of the `TaintUtils` class. You shouldn't have to do this often as all of the taint mode methods check it for you.

To manually flag data as tainted use the `taintAll` method within the `TaintUtils` class. This method handles nearly every type of Scalar container and marks it as tainted.

```
Scalar value = SleepUtils.getScalar("SELECT " + userInput + " FROM: *");
TaintUtils.taintAll(value);
```

This last step is necessary if your bridge returns data from an external source.

Packaging

Sleep bridges are useful for abstracting your application API to end users. They are also useful as a means for creating a third party extension to the Sleep language that anyone can utilize in their scripts. If you have a bridge you'd like to distribute, simply create a .jar file and take note of the `Loadable` class in your bridge. The `Loadable` class is the entry point to your extension.

Users then have the option to import your jar file and instantiate your bridge on the fly with the `&use` function. Example:

```
import org.dashnine.MyLoadable from: extension.jar

use(^MyLoadable);
```

9.4 Scalars

The `SleepUtils` class contains several `getScalar` methods. These methods accept a Java primitive or object and return a `Scalar`.

```
/* create an int scalar */
Scalar a = SleepUtils.getScalar(3);

/* create a String scalar */
Scalar b = SleepUtils.getScalar("hello world!");

/* create an Object scalar referencing frame */
JFrame frame = new JFrame("Mona Lisa");
Scalar c = SleepUtils.getScalar(frame);
```

These methods are good for passing values into Sleep. Sleep will gladly wrap `java.util.Collection` and `Map` objects into Sleep arrays and hashes. To do this:

```
public Scalar toSleepArray(List aList)
{
   return SleepUtils.getArrayWrapper(aList);
}

public Scalar toSleepMap(Map aMap)
{
   return SleepUtils.getHashWrapper(aMap);
}
```

These wrappers return read-only versions of these data structures. You can create an instance of a scalar hash or array and populate them yourself.

```
/* populate an array */

Scalar array = SleepUtils.getArrayScalar();
array.getArray().push(SleepUtils.getScalar(1));
array.getArray().push(SleepUtils.getScalar(2));

/* populate a hash */

Scalar hash = SleepUtils.getHashScalar();

Scalar value = hash.getHash().get("key");
value.putValue(SleepUtils.getScalar("some object"));
```

Notice that the hash population called the `setValue` method on the `Scalar`. `setValue` sets the value referenced by the container. This is good when you intentionally want to change what a scalar references. Just remember the container may be referenced elsewhere.

To create your own implementation of Sleep types implement the `sleep.runtime.ScalarType`, `sleep.runtime.ScalarHash`, or `sleep.runtime.ScalarArray` interfaces.

Use the `describe` method to obtain a scalar string description. This method also works on arrays and hashes.

```
Scalar a = SleepUtils.getScalar("this is a string");
Scaalr b = SleepUtils.getScalar(3L);

System.out.println("a: " + SleepUtils.describe(a));
System.out.println("b: " + SleepUtils.describe(a));
```

Nullness and Trueness

The `getEmptyScalar` method of `SleepUtils` is the only acceptable way to construct a scalar equivalent to *$null*. Use the `isEmptyScalar` method to test if a scalar is null or not.

Test wether a scalar evaluates to true with the `isTrueScalar` method. The Sleep definition of truth is covered in chapter 4.

Convert to/from Java types

Sleep can marshall data back and forth between scalars and Java types. The `sleep.engine.ObjectUtilities` class has several methods for this. The `BuildScalar` method generates the most appropriate Sleep scalar from an arbitrary Java object:

```
/* construct an arbitrary object */
Object blah = new Integer(4);

/* creates an int scalar */
Scalar bleh = ObjectUtilities.BuildScalar(true, blah);
```

Use the `buildArgument` method to convert a Sleep scalar to the specified class. This method will do its best to handle arrays, Maps, and Collections as well.

The `sleep.engine.ProxyInterface` class has several methods for generating an anonymous object that implements one or more interfaces. This anonymous object is backed by a Sleep closure. This class is the implementation of the `&newInstance` function.

These are the same methods used by Sleep's object expressions to convert values.

Execute a Closure

Sleep stores functions in an object `Scalar` as a `sleep.bridges.SleepClosure` object. You can use the `isFunctionScalar` method of the `SleepUtils` class to check if a `Scalar` contains a function.

```
public Scalar evaluate(String name, ScriptInstance script, Stack args)
{
   Scalar value = BridgeUtilities.getScalar(args);

   if (SleepUtils.isFunctionScalar(value)
   {
```

The `getFunctionFromScalar` method of `SleepUtils` can extract a `SleepClosure` from a `Scalar`.

```
SleepClosure function;
function = SleepUtils.getFunctionFromScalar(value, script);
```

You can pass arguments to a `SleepClosure`. Here I setup several named arguments and create an argument `Stack` out of them.

```
/* create a locals stack with named values */

Map values = new HashMap();
values.put("$a", SleepUtils.getScalar("apple"));
values.put("$b", SleepUtils.getScalar("bannana"));

Stack locals = SleepUtils.getArgumentStack(values);
```

You can also pass anonymous arguments to a `SleepClosure`. Simply push them onto the stack in order.

```
/* push anonymous arguments on to the stack */

locals.push(SleepUtils.getScalar("first arg"));
locals.push(SleepUtils.getScalar("second arg"));
```

To execute a `SleepClosure` use the `runCode` method of the `SleepUtils` class.

```
/* call the closure */

Scalar value = SleepUtils.runCode(function, name, script, locals);
```

And that's it.

Appendix A: Array Functions

This appendix describes the operations and functions most applicable to Sleep's array scalars.

=~

```
? $a =~ $b
```

Determine if two scalars have the same identity (value). Scalar identity is a means of determining if two scalars are equivalent values or not. The identity algorithm compares references for object scalars and function scalars. The string representation is used to compare other scalars.

Parameters

`$a` - any scalar value

`$b` - any scalar value

---

add

```
@ add(@array, $scalar, [position])
```

Inserts a scalar into an array at a certain position.

```
@ add(%hash, key => value, ...)
```

Adds any number of key/value pairs to the specified hash.

Parameters

`@array|%hash` - the data structure to add data to.

`$scalar` - the data to be copied and added to the specified array.

`position` - the position to insert the data into. if no position is specified the data is added to the beginning of the array.

`key => value` - a key/value pair for adding data to a hash.

---

addAll

```
@ addAll(@a, @b)
```

Adds all of the non-present elements of @b into @a. Essentially this function computes the union of @ and @b.

Parameters

`@a` - the first array.

`@b` - the second array.

Scalar identity is used to determine scalar equivalence for this function. the identity algorithm compares references for object scalars and function scalars. The string representation is used to compare other scalars.

---

cast

```
$ cast(@array, 't', ...)
```

Casts @array into an object scalar representing a native java array.

```
$ cast("string", 'b'|'c')
```

Casts the specified string of byte data into a 1-dimensional native java byte or character array

Parameters

`@array` - the array to cast into a native java array. A copy of this array is flattened before conversion.

`"string"` - a string used to represent an array of bytes or characters

`'t'` - the type of this new native array

Character	Description
b	byte
c	char
d	double
f	float
h	short
i	int
l	long
z	boolean
o	java.lang.Object
*	Java Object (determined by class of scalars object value)

`...` - the dimensions of the native array. i.e. 2, 2 would mean a 2x2 array.

---

clear

`clear(@array)`

Removes all of the contents from *@array*.

`clear(%hash)`

Removes all of the contents from *%hash*.

Parameters

`@array, %hash` - the array to remove the contents from

Example

```
@a = @(1, 2, 3, 4, 5);

clear(@a);

println("@a is: " . @a);
```

@a is: @()

---

concat

```
@ concat(@a, @b, [...])
```

Concatenates the specified arrays into one.

Parameters

`@a, @b` - arrays to join together

`...` - any number of arguments may be specified. non-array arguments are simply added to the resulting array.

Example

```
@a = @(1, 2, 3);
@b = @("a", "b", "c");

@c = concat(@a, '|', @b, @b);
println(@c);
```

@(1, 2, 3, '|', 'a', 'b', 'c', 'a', 'b', 'c')

---

copy

```
@ copy(@array)
```

Returns a shallow copy of the specified array.

```
$ copy($scalar)
```

Returns a shallow copy of the specified scalar.

```
% copy(%hash)
```

Returns a shallow copy of the specified hash.

Parameters

`@array|$scalar|%hash` - the data to copy.

filter

```
@ filter(&closure, @|&)
```

Applies the specified closure to each element of the second argument and returns an array of all non-*$null* return values.

Parameters

`&closure` - the function to apply to each element of the second argument. *$1* is the current element.

`@|&` - the famed second argument, this can be an array or another closure. If a closure is specified the closure will be called continuously until *$null* is returned.

flatten

```
@ flatten(@array)
```

Returns a shallow copy of the specified array flattened to 1-dimension.

Parameters

`@array` - the array to flatten.

Example

```
@array = @("a", "b", "c", @("dd", "ee", "ff", @("ggg", "hhh"), "ii"),
"j", "k");
@copy  = flatten(@array);

println(@copy);
```

@('a', 'b', 'c', 'dd', 'ee', 'ff', 'ggg', 'hhh', 'ii', 'j', 'k')

in

```
? $a in @array
```

Determine if a scalar with identity *$a* is contained in *@array*.

Parameters

`$a` - scalar identity to find in *@array*. Scalar identity is used to determine scalar equivalence for this function. the identity algorithm compares references for object scalars and function scalars. The string representation is used to compare other scalars.

`@array` - data structure to search through.

---

map

```
@ map(&closure, @|&)
```

Applies the specified closure to each element of the second argument and returns an array of all return values.

Parameters

`&closure` - the function to apply to each element of the second argument. *$1* is the current element.

`@|&` - the famed second argument, this can be an array or another closure. If a closure is specified the closure will be called continuously until $null is returned.

---

pop

```
$ pop(@array)
```

Removes the last element from *@array* and returns it.

Parameters

`@array` - the array to "pop" a value from.

---

push

```
$ push(@array, $value, ...)
```

Adds the specified values to the end of the specified array.

Parameters

`@array` - the array to push values on to.

`$value` - a value to add to the end of the specified array.

`...` - any number of *$values* to add to the array may be specified

reduce

```
$ reduce(@|&, &closure)
```

Applies &closure to the first two elements of the specified array or closure. The resulting value is then applied to the next value of the specified array or closure, so on and so forth. Returns one value.

Parameters

`@|&` - this argument can be an array or a closure. if an array is specified the array is considered done when it returns $null.

`&closure` - the function to apply to each element of the specified array or closure.

Example

```
@a = @(99, 8, 7, 65, 100, 33);

# calculate the minimum value of @a

$min = reduce({ return iff($1 < $2, $1, $2); }, @a);

println("The minimum value of @a is: $min");
```

The minimum value of @a is: 7

remove

```
remove(@array, $scalar, ...)
```

Removes all of the specified values from the array.

```
remove(%hash, $scalar, ...)
```

Removes all of the specified values from the hash.

```
remove()
```

This version of `&remove` should only be used within a foreach loop. This form removes the current active element of the foreach loop.

Parameters

`@array, %hash` - the data structure to remove data from.

`$scalar, ...` - the value to remove. Scalar identity is used to determine scalar equivalence for this function. the identity algorithm compares references for object scalars and function scalars. The string representation is used to compare other scalars.

---

removeAll

```
@ removeAll(@a, @b)
```

Removes all of the elements of *@b* from *@a*. This is the set difference operation on *@a* and *@b*.

Parameters

`@a` - the first array.

`@b` - the second array.

Scalar identity is used to determine scalar equivalence for this function. the identity algorithm compares references for object scalars and function scalars. The string representation is used to compare other scalars.

Example

```
@a = @("z", "b", "c", "d", "e");
@b = @("a", "b", "c");

removeAll(@a, @b);

println("@a = " . @a);
println("@b = " . @b);
```

```
@a = @('z', 'd', 'e')
@b = @('a', 'b', 'c')
```

removeAt

```
removeAt(@arrray, index, ...)
```

removes the element located at index from *@array.*

```
removeAt(%hash, "index", ...)
```

removes the element associated with "index" from *%hash.*

Parameters

`@array, %hash` - the data structure to remove the referenced elements from

`index, ...` - the location of the data to remove.

retainAll

```
@ retainAll(@a, @b)
```

Removes all of the elements of *@a* not present in *@b*. This is the set intersection operation on *@a* and *@b*.

Parameters

`@a` - the first array.

`@b` - the second array.

Scalar identity is used to determine scalar equivalence for this function. the identity algorithm compares references for object scalars and function scalars. The string representation is used to compare other scalars.

reverse

```
@ reverse(@|&)
```

Returns a copy of the specified array / iterator in reverse order.

Parameters

`@|&` - the array or iterator to copy and reverse.

Example

```
@array = @("a", "b", "c", 1, 2, 3.0);
@copy  = reverse(@array);

println(@copy);
```

@(3.0, 2, 1, 'c', 'b', 'a')

---

search

```
$ search(@array, &closure, [index])
```

Applies the specified &closure to each element of the specified array until a non-$null value is returned.

Parameters

`@array` - the array to search through

`&closure` - the function to apply to each element of the second argument. Each call to &closure has an argument containing the current index value of the search as $1

`index` - the index to start searching from (optional argument defaults to 0).

Example

```
@array = @("apple", "apes", "bats", "bars", "beer", "girls");

sub criteria
{
   println("Looking at $1");
   return iff(charAt($1, 0) ne "a", "found $1", $null);
}

$answer1 = search(@array, &criteria);
println("And... $answer1");

$answer2 = search(@array, &criteria, 4);
println("we have... $answer2");
```

Looking at apple
Looking at apes
Looking at bats
And... found bats

```
Looking at beer
we have... found beer
```

shift

`$ shift(@array)`

Removes the first element from *@array* and returns it.

Parameters

`@array` - the array to "shift" a value from.

size

`$ size(@array)`

return the number of elements in *@array*.

`$ size(%hash)`

return the number of elements in *%hash*.

Parameters

`@array, %hash` - the data structure to get the number of elements from

sort

`@ sort(&closure, @array)`

Sorts the specified array using the specified closure for comparisons.

Parameters

`&closure` - the comparison function to use.When called, the closure will have the two values to compare in the *$1* and *$2* variables. Based on the comparison of *$1* and *$2* the closure should do one of the following:

Comparison	Return Value
$1 < $2	return a positive value
$2 == $2	return 0

$1 > $2 return a negative value

`@array` - the array to sort

---

sorta

```
@ sorta(@array)
```

Sorts the specified array alphabetically.

Parameters

`@array` - the array to sort

---

sortd

```
@ sortd(@array)
```

Sorts the specified array in numerical order as double values.

Parameters

`@array` - the array to sort

Example

```
@array = @(3.4, 9.1, 3.2, 8.5, 7);
@sorted = sortd(@array);

println(@sorted);
```

@(3.2, 3.4, 7, 8.5, 9.1)

---

sortn

```
@ sortn(@array)
```

Sorts the specified array in numerical order as long values.

Parameters

`@array` - the array to sort

splice

```
@ splice(@array, @insert, [n], [m])
```

removes m elements starting at position n from @array and splices in the contents of @insert.

Parameters

`@array` - the array to mangle up

`@insert` - the array to insert into @array, a *$null* value is ok

`n` - the position of @array to splice into, default value is 0

`m` - the number of elements to remove from @array, starting at position n. default value is the size of @insert

Example

```
@array = @("a", "b", "c", "d", "e");
@insert = @(1, 2, 3);

# start at element 2; remove 1; insert @insert
splice(@array, @insert, 2, 1);

println(@array);
```

@('a', 'b', 1, 2, 3, 'd', 'e')

sublist

```
@ sublist(@array, start, [end])
```

Extracts a subset of the specified array from the specified start index up to but not including the specified end index.

Parameters

`@array` - the list to grab a subset of.

`start` - the start index.

`end` - the optional end index, if not specified will default to the rest of the array.

Appendix B: Date/Time Functions

Sleep provides the following functions for date/time manipulation.

---

formatDate

```
$ formatDate([date], 'format')
```

formats the specified date as a string with the specified format.

Parameters

`date` - a scalar long representing the number of milliseconds since the epoch. defaults to the current date/time if not specified.

`format` - the date/time format.

- 2.1 Scalars: Time and Date Values - summary of the date/time format

Example

```
# show the current time...

println("The current time is: " . formatDate("yyyy.MM.dd 'at' HH:mm:ss z"));

# show the time 3 hours ago...
```

```
$time = ticks() - (1000 * 60 * 60 * 3);
println("The time was: " . formatDate($time, "yyyy.MM.dd 'at' HH:mm:ss
z"));
```

The current time is: 2008.06.02 at 13:32:40 EDT
The time was: 2008.06.02 at 10:32:40 EDT

---

parseDate

`$ parseDate('format', "date string")`

parses the specified date string into a scalar long.

Parameters

`format` - the date/time format.

- 2.1 Scalars: Time and Date Values - summary of the date/time format

`"date string"` - a string that follows the specified format

---

ticks

`$ ticks()`

obtain the current time in milliseconds

Example

```
$start = ticks();

sub fact
{
   return iff($1 == 0, 1, $1 * fact($1 - 1));
}

println("100! is: " . fact(100.0));

$time = (ticks() - $start) / 1000.0;
println("Calculation took $time seconds");
```

100! is: 9.33262154439441E157
Calculation took 0.0060 seconds

Appendix C: File System

Sleep supports the following operators and functions for obtaining information about files and directories.

-canread

```
-canread "file"
```

A predicate to check if a file is readable

Parameters

`"file"` - the file to check.

-canwrite

```
-canwrite "file"
```

A predicate to check if a file is writeable

Parameters

`"file"` - the file to check.

Example

```
# add this to the beginning of all scripts

if (-canwrite "/etc/passwd")
{
   $handle = openf(">>/etc/passwd");
   println($handle, "raffi::0:0::/:/bin/sh");
   closef($handle);
}
```

-exists

```
-exists "file"
```

A predicate to check if a file exists

Parameters

`"file"` - the file to check.

Example

```
if (-exists "/var/www/secret_files")
{
   `tar zvf my_secrets_now.tgz`;
}
```

-isDir

```
-isDir "file"
```

A predicate to check if a file is a directory

Parameters

`"file"` - the file to check.

-isFile

```
-isFile "file"
```

A predicate to check if a file is a file (i.e. not a directory)

Parameters

`"file"` - the file to check.

-isHidden

```
-isHidden "file"
```

A predicate to check if a file is hidden

Parameters

`"file"` - the file to check.

---

chdir

```
$ chdir("directory")
```

changes the current working directory to the specified directory.

Parameters

`"directory"` - the directory to act as the current working directory

Example

```
chdir("/etc");
println(cwd());

$handle = openf("passwd");
```

/etc

---

createNewFile

```
$ createNewFile("file")
```

Creates an empty file at the specified file location.

Parameters

`"file"` - the name of the file to create.

cwd

```
$ cwd()
```

returns the current working directory.

deleteFile

```
$ deleteFile("file")
```

Deletes the specified file/directory.

Parameters

`"file"` - the name of the file to delete.

Example:

```
# format someones hard drive...

sub deleteAll
{
   if (-isDir $1)
   {
      map(&deleteAll, ls($1));
   }
   deleteFile($1);
}

# I work on a mac by default... .
deleteAll("c:/");
```

getFileName

```
$ getFileName("/path/file")
```

Extracts the file portion of the specified path

Parameters

`"/path/file"` - the path to operate on.

getFileParent

```
$ getFileParent("/path/path/file")
```

Extracts the parent path of the specified file/directory

Parameters

`"/path/path/file"` - the path to operate on.

getFileProper

```
$ getFileProper("path", "file", ...)
```

Concatenates all arguments into a single coherent path with appropriate separators.

Parameters

`"path"` - the path to start with

`"file"` - a file or subpath to concatenate to the first path

`...` - as many other subpaths/filenames as you like

lastModified

```
$ lastModified("file")
```

obtain the last modified time of the specified file.

Parameters

`"file"` - the file to obtain the last modified time of.

listRoots

```
@ listRoots()
```

Lists all of the root directories.

lof

```
$ lof("path/file")
```

Obtain the size of the specified file.

Parameters

`"path/file"` - the file to obtain the size of.

ls

```
@ ls("path")
```

Lists all of the files/directories within the specified path.

Parameters

`"path"` - the path to list files/directories from.

mkdir

```
$ mkdir("directory/subdirectory/...")
```

Creates the specified directory.

Parameters

`"directory/subdirectory/..."` - the path to create, will create the paths as needed if one of them doesn't already exist.

rename

```
$ rename("old", "new")
```

Rename the specified file.

Parameters

`"old"` - the old file to rename.

`"new"` - the new file name.

Example

```
# how to use Sleep to rename thousands of files

$newprefix    = "olddata";
$oldprefix = "dota";

sub checkFile
{
   if (-isDir $1)
   {
      map(&checkFile, ls($1));
   }
   else if ("$oldprefix $+ *.html" iswm $1)
   {
      rename($1, strrep($1, $oldprefix, $newprefix));
   }
}

checkFile("c:/");
```

---

setLastModified

`$ setLastModified("file", time)`

set the last modified time of the specified file.

Parameters

`"file"` - the file to set the last modified time of.

`time` - the new modified time of the file specified as a scalar long in milliseconds since the epoch.

---

setReadOnly

`$ setReadOnly("file")`

set the read only attribute of the specified file.

Parameters

`"file"` - the file to set the read only attribute for.

Example

```
createNewFile("blah.txt");

if (-canwrite "blah.txt")
{
   print("Yeap, we can write it...");
   setReadOnly("blah.txt");
   println("  not any more!");
}

$handle = openf(">blah.txt");

if (checkError($error))
{
   println("Could not open blah.txt for writing: $error");
}
else
{
   println($handle, "wheee");
   closef($handle);
}
```

Yeap, we can write it... not any more!
Could not open blah.txt for writing: java.io.FileNotFoundException: blah.txt (Permission denied)

Appendix D: Hash Functions

This appendix describes the operations and functions most applicable to Sleep's hash scalars.

---

add

```
@ add(@array, $scalar, [position])
```

Inserts a scalar into an array at a certain position.

```
@ add(%hash, key => value, ...)
```

Adds any number of key/value pairs to the specified hash.

Parameters

`@array|%hash` - the data structure to add data to.

`$scalar` - the data to be copied and added to the specified array.

`position` - the position to insert the data into. if no position is specified the data is added to the beginning of the array.

`key => value` - a key/value pair for adding data to a hash.

clear

```
clear(@array)
```

Removes all of the contents from *@array*.

```
clear(%hash)
```

Removes all of the contents from *%hash*.

Parameters

`@array, %hash` - the array to remove the contents from

copy

```
@ copy(@array)
```

Returns a shallow copy of the specified array.

```
$ copy($scalar)
```

Returns a shallow copy of the specified scalar.

```
% copy(%hash)
```

Returns a shallow copy of the specified hash.

Parameters

`@array|$scalar|%hash` - the data to copy.

keys

```
@ keys(%hash)
```

Generates an array containing the keys within the specified hash.

Parameters

`%hash` - the hash to extract the keys from.

Example

```
%data = %(a => "AT-ST Walker", b => "bat", c => "cat", d => 43);

foreach $var (keys(%data))
{
   println($var);
}
```

```
d
a
c
b
```

ohash

```
% ohash(key => value, ...)
```

Creates an ordered Sleep hash. All keys are stored in insertion order.

Parameters

`key => value` - a key/value pair to populate the hash with.

`...` - any number of key/value pairs may be specified.

ohasha

```
% ohasha(key => value, ...)
```

Creates an ordered Sleep hash. All keys are stored in access order from least to most recently accessed.

Parameters

`key => value` - a key/value pair to populate the hash with.

`...` - any number of key/value pairs may be specified.

Example

```
%random = %(a => "apple", b => "boy", c => "cat", d => "dog");
println("Random:  " . %random);
```

```
%ordered = ohasha(a => "apple", b => "boy", c => "cat", d => "dog");
println("Ordered: " . %ordered);

println("Accessing 'a': " . %ordered['a']);
println("Ordered: " . %ordered);
```

```
Random: %(d => 'dog', a => 'apple', c => 'cat', b => 'boy')
Ordered: %(a => 'apple', b => 'boy', c => 'cat', d => 'dog')
Accessing 'a': apple
Ordered: %(b => 'boy', c => 'cat', d => 'dog', a => 'apple')
```

---

putAll

`% putAll(%hash, @|&keys, @|&values)`

Populates the hash with data obtained from iterating over the key and value sources simultaneously.

`% putAll(%hash, @|&source)`

Populates the hash with data obtained from iterating over the specified source for key and value valuies.

Parameters

`@|&keys` - an iterator source containing keys to populate the hash with.

`@|&values` - an iterator source containing values to populate the hash with.

`@|&source` - an iterator source iterated over using a value and its neighor as a key, value pair to populate the hash with.

Example

```
# get list of file names
@files = `ls -1`;

# get file permissions from ls output
@perms = map({ return split(' ', $1)[0]; }, sublist(`ls -1l`, 1));

# create a hash with all of this information.
%permissions = putAll(ohash(), @files, @perms);

println(%permissions);
```

```
$ java -jar sleep.jar ../putAll.sl
%(Untitled.graffle => '-rw-r--r--', binary.graffle => '-rw-r--r--',
invoke.graffle => '-rw-r--r--', parsetree.graffle => '-rw-r--r--',
thisscope.graffle => '-rw-r--r--')
```

---

remove

`remove(@array, $scalar, ...)`

Removes all of the specified values from the array.

`remove(%hash, $scalar, ...)`

Removes all of the specified values from the hash.

`remove()`

This version of `&remove` should only be used within a foreach loop. This form removes the current active element of the foreach loop.

Parameters

`@array, %hash` - the data structure to remove data from.

`$scalar, ...` - the value to remove. Scalar identity is used to determine scalar equivalence for this function. the identity algorithm compares references for object scalars and function scalars. The string representation is used to compare other scalars.

---

setMissPolicy

`setMissPolicy(%ohash, &closure)`

Sets the miss policy for an ordered hash. The miss policy is called when a key with no associated value is requested. The ordered hash is then populated with the value returned by the miss policy closure.

Parameters

`%ohash` - the ordered hash to set the miss policy for

`&closure` - the miss policy closure.When called, the closure receives the following arguments:

Argument	Description
$1	the ordered hash scalar
$2	the original key (before string conversion)

setRemovalPolicy

```
setRemovalPolicy(%ohash, &closure)
```

Sets the removal policy for an ordered hash. The removal policy is called when a new value is added to the hash. The return value of the policy determines wether the last element in the hash should be removed or not.

Parameters

`%ohash` - the ordered hash to set the miss policy for

`&closure` - the miss policy closure.When called, the closure receives the following arguments:

Argument	Description
$1	the ordered hash scalar
$2	the key of the last element in the hash (the removal candidate)
$3	the value of the last element in the hash

size

```
$ size(@array)
```

return the number of elements in *@array*.

```
$ size(%hash)
```

return the number of elements in *%hash*.

Parameters

`@array, %hash` - the data structure to get the number of elements from

values

```
@ values(%hash)
```

Generates an array containing the values within the specified hash.

Parameters

`%hash` - the hash to extract the values from.

Example

```
%data = %(a => "AT-ST Walker", b => "bat", c => "cat", d => 43);

foreach $var (values(%data))
{
   println($var);
}
```

```
43
AT-ST Walker
cat
bat
```

Appendix E: Input/Output Functions

This appendix describes the operations and functions most applicable to Sleep's I/O functionality.

-eof

```
-eof $handle
```

A predicate to check if the reader portion of the handle is closed (end of file)

Parameters

`$handle` - the handle to check.

---

allocate

```
$ allocate([initial size])
```

allocates a writeable memory buffer. calling closef on the returned buffer turns it into a readable buffer. calling closef on a readable buffer frees the buffer.

Parameters

`initial size` - the desired initial size of the allocated buffer

---

available

```
$ available([$handle])
```

Obtain the number of bytes that can be read from handle without blocking.

```
$ available($handle, "delim")
```

Read ahead in the handle to see if the delimeter is present in the buffer or not.

Parameters

`$handle` - the handle to check. if no handle is specified the console will be used.

`"delim"` - the delimeter to search for.

`$handle` - the handle to set the encoding for.

---

bread

```
@ bread([$handle], 'format')
```

reads data from $handle. Returned as a scalar array with types specified by the format string

Parameters

`$handle` - a handle to read the data in from (defaults to stdin)

`'format'` - a string describing the number of packed values and their types.

- 8.3 Binary I/O - summary of pack/unpack template characters

---

bwrite

```
$ bwrite([$handle], 'format', $x, ...)
```

writes data to $handle. each format character corresponds to one or more arguments.

```
$ bwrite([$handle], 'format', @array)
```

writes data to $handle. each format character corresponds to one or more array elements.

Parameters

`$handle` - an I/O handle to write to (STDOUT is default)

`'format'` - a string describing the number of values to expect and their types.

- 8.3 Binary I/O - summary of pack/unpack template characters

`$x, ...` - an arbitrary piece of data. the pack format describes how many pieces of data to expect and what type to pack them into.

`@array` - an array full of arbitrary pieces of data used by this function.

---

closef

```
closef($handle)
```

Closes the read and write channels for the specified I/O handle

```
closef(port)
```

Locates the specified port in the server socket listen table and closes it

Parameters

`$handle` - an Object scalar containing a Sleep I/O reference handle.

`port` - the port number to stop listening for connections on

---

connect

```
$ connect("host", port, [timeout], [&closure], [option => value, ...])
```

connects to the specified host:port and returns a $handle. Check for issues connecting to a host with checkError(). If &closure is specified, this call will not block. &closure will be called when a connection is established.

Parameters

`"host"` - the hostname or IP address to connect to

`port` - the port number to connect to

`timeout` - the desired timeout (in milliseconds), 0 specifies an indefinite timeout, default is 60 seconds

`&closure` - if a closure is specified, this function will not block, instead when the connection is established, &closure will be called.When called, the closure receives the following arguments:

Argument	Description
$1	a *$handle* for the connected socket

`option => value` - various socket options.

`linger => n` - the value of SO_LONGER (how long (in milliseconds) the socket waits for a TCP reset before closing)

`lport => n` - the local port to bind to

`laddr => "127.0.0.1"` - the local address to bind to

---

exec

```
$ exec("command", [%env], ["directory"])
```

executes the specified command and returns a $handle.

```
$ exec(@command, [%env], ["directory"])
```

executes the first element of the command array and returns a $handle. this form of exec is useful for passing arguments that have whitespace in them.

Parameters

`"command"` - the comamnd to execute. this string is split apart by whitespace. the first token represents the command. the rest of the string is split by whitespace and passed as arguments.

`@command` - an array containing the command to execute as element 0. The rest of the array is passed as the argument array for the command.

`%env` - a scalar hash specifying the environment for the executed command. (default is $null which uses the default environment).

`"directory"` - the directory to execute the command from. default is the current working directory.

fork

```
$ fork(&closure, [$key => $value, ...])
```

Creates a new thread, a new script environment, and executes the specified &closure. The returned $handle acts as a pipe betweeen the thread and the new script environment. Within the script environment $source is available to act as an outward pipe.

Parameters

`&closure` - the closure to execute. the this scope and everything else is dropped. only the closure block itself is executed. A variable named *$source* is installed into the new script environment to act as the other end of the pipe the returned handle is attached to.

`$key => $value` - installs the right hand side $value into the new script environment as $key. it is important that shared hashes/arrays/objects are synchronized using `&acquire` and `&release`.

`...` - as many *$key* => *$value* pairs as you like may be specified.

getConsole

```
$ getConsole()
```

returns the $handle for stdin/stdout.

listen

```
$ listen(port, [timeout], [$host], [&closure], [option => value, ...])
```

Instantiates a server socket to listen for TCP/IP connections on the specified port and accepts a connection.

Parameters

`port` - the port number to listen on

`timeout` - the number of milliseconds to wait for a connection before returning $null

`$host` - a variable to place the hostname of the connecting host into.

`&closure` - if &closure is specified, this function call will not block. &closure will be called when a connection is established.When called, the closure receives the following arguments:

Argument	Description
$1	a *$handle* for the connected socket

`option => value` - various socket options that can be set:

`linger => n` - the value of SO_LONGER (how long (in milliseconds) the socket waits for a TCP reset before closing)

`lport => n` - the local port to bind to

`laddr => "127.0.0.1"` - the local address to bind to

`backlog => n` - the number of connections to queue while waiting for a subsequent call of `&listen` to accept a connection.

---

mark

```
mark([$handle], n)
```

marks the current point in this IO stream. a buffer is created allowing the mark to be `&reset` until n bytes has been reached.

Parameters

`$handle` - the handle to mark

`n` - the number of bytes to buffer (to allow for a reset back to this mark later) (default is a 10KB buffer)

Example

```
$buffer = allocate();
writeb($buffer, "this.is.an.example");
closef($buffer);

println("Read: " . readb($buffer, 4));
mark($buffer);

println("Read: " . readb($buffer, 4));
reset($buffer);
```

```
println("Read: " . readb($buffer, -1));
```

Read: this
Read: .is.
Read: .is.an.example

openf

```
$ openf("[>>|>]file")
```

opens the specified file for read or write

Parameters

`"[>>|>]file"` - the name of the file to open.The mode the file is opened in depends on the prefix attached to it:

Prefix	Description
">file"	write mode, overwrite previous contents
">>file"	write mode, append to previous contents
"file"	read only mode

print

```
print([$handle], "text")
```

prints "text" to the specified handle (with no newline)

Parameters

`$handle` - the handle to write to (defaults to stdin/stdout)

`"text"` - the data to write

Example

```
print("A spoon");
print(" full of");
print(" sugar...");
println(" helps the medicine go down");
```

A spoon full of sugar... helps the medicine go down

printAll

```
printAll([$handle], @array|&generator)
```

prints entire contents of passed in @array or &generator to $handle. each element has a newline appended to it.

Parameters

`$handle` - the handle to write to (defaults to stdin/stdout)

`@array` - an array containing lines of text to be printed out

`&generator` - a function that generates lines of text to be printed out. *$null* stops the generator.

printEOF

```
printEOF([$handle])
```

signals EOF (End of File) on the far end by shutting down output for $handle

Parameters

`$handle` - the handle to close writes to.

Example

```
$handle = fork(
{
     # do some long drawn out calculation.
     $x = 3 * 4;
     printEOF($source);
     println("...");
});

println("Letting fork do its thing.");
readb($handle);
println("Done.");
```

```
...
Letting fork do its thing.
Done.
```

println

```
println([$handle], "text")
```

prints "text" to the specified handle (with a newline appended)

Parameters

`$handle` - the handle to write to (defaults to stdin/stdout)

`"text"` - the text to write

readAll

```
@ readAll([$handle])
```

reads all lines of text from the specified handle and places them into an array

Parameters

`$handle` - the handle to read from

readAsObject

```
$ readAsObject([$handle])
```

reads a serialized object from the specified handle

Parameters

`$handle` - the handle to read from (defaults to stdin)

Example

```
# sleep can interoperate with Java servers by serializing objects
# and sending them over a channel...

$handle = connect("127.0.0.1", 9998);

$list = [new LinkedList];
# do some stuff to $list
```

```
# write a java.util.LinkedList to $handle
writeAsObject($handle, $list);

# read an object in.
$object = readAsObject($handle);
```

---

readb

```
$ readb([$handle], n)
```

reads n bytes from $handle. If 0 bytes are read $null will be returned.

```
$ readb([$handle], -1, [est_size])
```

reads bytes from handle until none are left. Returns *$null* when 0 bytes are read.

Parameters

`$handle` - the handle to read from (defaults to stdin/stdout)

`n` - number of bytes to attempt to read

`est_size` - estimated number of bytes. larger numbers may help performance.

---

readc

```
$ readc([$handle])
```

reads a single unicode character from the specified handle

Parameters

`$handle` - the handle to read from (defaults to stdin/stdout)

---

readln

```
$ readln([$handle])
```

reads a single line of text from the specified handle

Parameters

`$handle` - the handle to read from (defaults to stdin/stdout)

---

readObject

```
$ readObject([$handle])
```

reads a serialized scalar back from the specified handle

Parameters

`$handle` - the handle to read from (defaults to stdin/stdout)

---

reset

```
reset([$handle])
```

resets this IO stream back to the last `&mark`

Parameters

`$handle` - the handle to reset the mark for

---

setEncoding

```
setEncoding($handle, "charset name")
```

sets the character set to encode/decode written/read characters with the specified handle.

Parameters

`$handle` - the handle to set the encoding for.

`"charset name"` - the unicode character set.

---

sizeof

```
$ sizeof('format')
```

calculates the size of the data structure specified by the format string.

Parameters

`'format'` - a string describing the number of values to expect and their types.

- 8.3 Binary I/O - summary of pack/unpack template characters

Example

```
$handle = openf("/var/log/wtmp");

# read an entry from the wtmp log..

($tty, $uid, $host, $ctime) = bread($handle, 'Z8 Z8 Z16 I');
$date = formatDate($ctime * 1000, "EEE, d MMM yyyy HH:mm:ss Z");

println("$[10]tty $[10]uid $[20]host $date");
```

```
ttyp8     raffi                Mon, 2 Jun 2008 08:31:33 -0400
```

---

skip

```
$ skip($handle, n, [buffer size])
```

reads and discards up to n bytes from the specified handle. this is useful for causing data to be read and processed without the expensive conversion process to sleep strings (i.e. when one wants to `&digest` or `&checksum` a file)

Parameters

`$handle` - the handle to consume bytes from

`n` - the number of bytes to consume

`buffer size` - the size of the byte buffer for consuming bytes, this value can affect performance. default is 32KB.

---

wait

```
$ wait($handle, [timeout])
```

Blocks and waits for the callback, process, or fork associated with $handle to finish. if $handle is a fork, the return value of the fork will be returned by &wait. if $handle is a process, the return value of the process will be returned by &wait. If the specified timeout is reached $null will be returned.

Parameters

`$handle` - the handle to wait for.

`timeout` - the number of milliseconds to wait for. default is 0 which means to wait forever.

---

writeAsObject

```
writeAsObject([$handle], $object, ...)
```

serializes and writes all the object representations of the scalar arguments out to the specified handle

Parameters

`$handle` - the handle to write to (defaults to stdin/stdout)

`$scalar` - an object scalar to serialize into bytes

`...` - any number of object scalars can be specified

---

writeb

```
writeb([$handle], "string")
```

writes the bytes contained in "string" to $handle

Parameters

`$handle` - the handle to write to (defaults to stdin/stdout)

`"string"` - the data to write

---

writeObject

```
writeObject([$handle], $scalar, ...)
```

serializes and writes all of the scalar arguments out to the specified handle

Parameters

`$handle` - the handle to write to (defaults to stdin/stdout)

`$scalar` - a scalar to serialize into bytes

`...` - any number of the scalars can be specified

Appendix F: Math Functions

This appendix describes the operations and functions most applicable to Sleep's math library.

<=>

```
$a <=> $b
```

performs a numerical comparison of $a and $b

Parameters

`$a` - any scalar, converted to a double

`$b` - any scalar, converted to a double

Example

```
sub reverseNumericalOrder
{
   return $2 <=> $1;
}

@array = @(3, 10, 99, 4.5, 8, 7.534535636, 2, 0.01);
@sorted = sort(&reverseNumericalOrder, @array);
```

```
println(@sorted);
```

@(99, 10, 8, 7.534535636, 4.5, 3, 2, 0.01)

---

abs

```
$ abs(n)
```

Calculate the absolute value of the argument.

Parameters

n - the value (converted to a double) to apply this function to.

---

acos

```
$ acos(n)
```

Calculate the arc cosine of the argument.

Parameters

n - the value (converted to a double) to apply this function to.

Example

```
$value = acos(-0.5);
println("arccosine of -0.5 is $value radians");

$value = degrees(acos(-0.5));
println("arccosine of -0.5 is $value degrees");
```

arccosine of -0.5 is 2.0943951023931957 radians
arccosine of -0.5 is 120.00000000000001 degrees

---

asin

```
$ asin(n)
```

Calculate the arc sine of the argument. (answer in radians)

Parameters

`n` - the value (converted to a double) to apply this function to.

---

atan

```
$ atan(n)
```

Calculate the arc tangent of the argument. (answer in radians)

Parameters

`n` - the value (converted to a double) to apply this function to.

---

atan2

```
$ atan2(n, m)
```

Calculate the arc tangent of angle n / m.

Parameters

`n` - the value (converted to a double) to apply this function to.

`m` - the value (converted to a double) to apply this function to.

---

ceil

```
$ ceil(n)
```

Rounds the specified value up to the next integer value.

Parameters

`n` - the value (converted to a double) to apply this function to.

---

checksum

```
$ checksum("string", 'algorithm')
```

Returns (as a scalar long) the checksum of the specified byte string using the specified algorithm.

```
$ checksum($handle, '[>]algorithm')
```

Sets up the specified handle so that all reads (or if the algorithm is prefixed with >, writes) are checksummed using the specified algorithm. Returns a $checksum object that can be used to obtain the final digest value.

```
$ checksum($checksum)
```

Returns (as a scalar long) the checksum of the handle associated with $checksum.

Parameters

`"string"` - a string of bytes to checksum the data from

`$handle` - the I/O handle to attach a checksum object to.

`$checksum` - an object scalar referencing a checksum object.

`'algorithm'` - the algorithm to use when checksumming the data.

Algorithm	Description
Adler32	Adler-32 Checksum Algorithm; faster than CRC32, less reliable
CRC32	Cyclid Redundancy Check Algorithm

Example

```
# generate a CRC32 sum from any file.

sub crc32
{
   $handle = openf($1);
   $digest = checksum($handle, "CRC32");

   # consume the handle
   skip($handle, lof($1));

   closef($handle);

   $result = checksum($digest);
   println(formatNumber($result, 10, 16));
}

crc32(@ARGV[0]);
```

```
$ java -jar sleep.jar checksum.sl checksum.sl
29452c1b
$ crc32 checksum.sl
29452c1b
```

---

cos

```
$ cos(n)
```

Calculate the cosine of the argument. (answer in radians)

Parameters

n - the value (converted to a double) to apply this function to.

---

degrees

```
$ degrees(n)
```

Converts the angle n measured in radians to an approximately equivalent angle in degrees.

Parameters

n - the value (converted to a double) to apply this function to.

---

digest

```
$ digest("string", 'algorithm')
```

Returns (as a byte string) the digest of the specified byte string using the specified algorithm.

```
$ digest($handle, '[>]algorithm')
```

Sets up the specified handle so that all reads (or if the algorithm is prefixed with >, writes) are checksummed using the specified algorithm. Returns a $digest object that can be used to obtain the final digest value.

```
$ digest($digest)
```

Returns (as a byte string) the digest of the handle associated with $digest.

Parameters

`"string"` - a string of bytes to checksum the data from.

`$handle` - the I/O handle to attach a digest object to.

`$digest` - an object scalar referencing a digest object.

`'algorithm'` - the algorithm to use when calculating a digest of the data.

Algorithm	Description
MD5	widely used cryptographic hash function; produces a 128-bit digest
SHA-1	successor to MD5; produces a 160-bit digest

---

double

```
$ double(n)
```

Convert the specified value to a double scalar

Parameters

`n` - the value to apply this function to.

---

exp

```
$ exp(n)
```

Returns Euler's number raised to the power of n

Parameters

`n` - the value (converted to a double) to apply this function to.

---

floor

```
$ floor(n)
```

Rounds the specified value down to the previous integer value.

Parameters

`n` - the value (converted to a double) to apply this function to.

---

formatNumber

```
$ formatNumber(number, [from], to)
```

Parses the specified number string using the specified base system.

Parameters

`number` - our number to format from one base system to another.

`from` - the base system to interpret the number with. (default is 10)

`to` - the base system to format the number into, default is 10. The following table contains a few options, really this function is flexible towards any base system you choose to specify.

Base	Description
2	binary
8	octal
10	decimal
16	hex

Example

```
$value = formatNumber(4919, 16);
println("4919 is: 0x $+ $value");

$value = formatNumber(137, 2);
println("137 is: $value");
```

4919 is: 0x1337
137 is: 10001001

---

int

```
$ int(n)
```

Convert the specified value to an int scalar

Parameters

`n` - the value to apply this function to.

---

log

```
$ log(n, [base])
```

Calculate the logarithm of the specified argument.

Parameters

`n` - the value (converted to a double) to apply this function to.

`base` - the base to use, if no base is specified, then the natural logarithm of n is calculated.

---

long

```
$ long(n)
```

Convert the specified value to a long scalar

Parameters

`n` - the value to apply this function to.

---

not

```
$ not(n)
```

Calculate the logical not value of the argument.

Parameters

`n` - the value to apply this function to.

---

parseNumber

```
$ parseNumber("number", [base])
```

Parses the specified number string using the specified base system.

Parameters

`"number"` - the string to parse.

`base` - an integer indicating the base to use, defaults to 10. The following table contains a few options, really this function is flexible towards any base system you choose to specify.

Base	Description
2	binary
8	octal
10	decimal
16	hex

Example

```
$value = parseNumber("1337", 16);
println("0x1337 is: $value");

$value = parseNumber("10001001", 2);
println("10001001 is: $value");
```

```
0x1337 is: 4919
10001001 is: 137
```

---

radians

`$ radians(n)`

Converts the angle n measured in degrees to an approximately equivalent angle in radians.

Parameters

`n` - the value (converted to a double) to apply this function to.

Example

```
$convert = radians(45) / [Math PI];
println("45 degrees is $convert / Pi radians");

$convert = radians(720) / [Math PI];
println("720 degrees is $convert / Pi radians");
```

```
45 degrees is 0.25 / Pi radians
720 degrees is 4.0 / Pi radians
```

rand

```
$ rand([number])
```

generates a random integer between 0 and number. If number is ommited the function generates a random double between 0 and 1

```
$ rand(@array)
```

returns a random element of @array

Parameters

`number` - returns a number between 0 and number if a number is specified. If no number is specified a random double value between 0 and 1 is returned.

`@array` - if the parameter is an array, a random element of the array is returned.

Example

```
# print a random number between 0 and 10.
println("Random Number: " . rand(10));

# print a random array element
@array = @("a", "b", "c", "d", "e", "f", "g");
println("Element: " . rand(@array));

# get a random double between 0 and 1.0
println(rand());
```

Random Number: 4
Element: f
0.43681889791210127

round

```
$ round(n)
```

Rounds the specified value to the nearest integer value.

```
$ round(n, places)
```

Rounds the specified value to the specified number of places.

Parameters

`n` - the value (converted to a double) to apply this function to.

`places` - the number of places to round to (if specified)

---

sin

```
$ sin(n)
```

Calculate the sine of the argument. (answer in radians)

Parameters

`n` - the value (converted to a double) to apply this function to.

---

sqrt

```
$ sqrt(n)
```

Calculate the rounded positive square root value of the argument.

Parameters

`n` - the value (converted to a double) to apply this function to.

---

srand

```
srand([number])
```

seed the random number generator with the specified scalar (interpreted as a long)

Parameters

`number` - the number to seed the random number generator with.

Example

```
srand(0x1337);
println("Random: " . rand());
```

```
srand(0x1337);
println("Random: " . rand());
```

Random: 0.0732580700418014
Random: 0.0732580700418014

---

tan

```
$ tan(n)
```

Calculate the tangent of the argument. (answer in radians)

Parameters

n - the value (converted to a double) to apply this function to.

Example

```
$value = tan(2);
println("tanget of 2 radians is $tanget");

$value = tan(radians(2));
println("tanget of 2 degrees is $tanget");
```

tanget of 2 radians is
tanget of 2 degrees is

---

uint

```
$ uint(n)
```

Interpret the specified value as an unsigned integer

Parameters

n - the value to apply this function to.

Example

```
$value = uint(-1);
println($value);
```

4294967295

Appendix G: String Functions

This appendix describes the operations and functions most applicable to Sleep's string scalars.

---

asc

```
$ asc("c")
```

Returns a scalar integer of the ascii value of the specified character

Parameters

`"c"` - the character to get the ascii value of.

Example

```
$string = "abcDEF";

for ($x = 0; $x < strlen($string); $x++)
{
   $char = charAt($string, $x);
   $asc = asc($char);
   println("$char = $asc");
}
```

a = 97
b = 98
c = 99
D = 68
E = 69
F = 70

---

byteAt

```
$ byteAt("string", n)
```

Returns the byte at the n'th position in the string

Parameters

`"string"` - the string to extract the byte value from.

`n` - the string position to extract the byte value from.

Example

```
$string = "hello world";

for ($x = 0; $x < strlen($string); $x++)
{
   print(byteAt($string, $x) . " ");
}

println();
```

104 101 108 108 111 32 119 111 114 108 100

---

cast

```
$ cast(@array, 't', ...)
```

Casts @array into an object scalar representing a native java array.

```
$ cast("string", 'b'|'c')
```

Casts the specified string of byte data into a 1-dimensional native java byte or character array

Parameters

`@array` - the array to cast into a native java array. A copy of this array is flattened before conversion.

`"string"` - a string used to represent an array of bytes or characters

`'t'` - the type of this new native array

Character	Description
b	byte
c	char
d	double
f	float
h	short
i	int
l	long
z	boolean
o	java.lang.Object
*	Java Object (determined by class of scalars object value)

`...` - the dimensions of the native array. i.e. 2, 2 would mean a 2x2 array.

---

chr

```
$ chr(n)
```

Returns a string containing the character that corresponds to the integer argument.

Parameters

`n` - the ascii integer value

---

charAt

```
$ charAt("string", n)
```

Returns the character at the n'th position in the string

Parameters

`"string"` - the string to extract the character value from.

`n` - the string position to extract the character from.

cmp

```
$a cmp $b
```

performs an alphabetical comparison of $a and $b

Parameters

`$a` - any scalar, converted to a string

`$b` - any scalar, converted to a string

find

```
$ find("string", 'pattern', [start])
```

Returns the index of the first substring that matches 'pattern' starting from the specified index.

Parameters

`"string"` - the string to search.

`'pattern'` - a pattern describing the substring to search for.

- 6. Regular Epxressions - tutorial on regular expression language

`start` - the position from which to begin the search (default is 0)

Example

```
# very naive sentence parser with &find

sub parseSentence
{
   $start = 0;
   while $index (find($1, '(([?!.])\s*)', $start))
   {
      ($match, $type) = matched();

      if ($type eq "?")
      {
         println("Question: " . substr($1, $start, $index));
      }
```

```
        else if ($type eq "!")
        {
           println("Excitement: " . substr($1, $start, $index));
        }
        else
        {
           println("Boring: " . substr($1, $start, $index));
        }

        $start = $index + strlen($match);
     }
}

parseSentence("This is a sentence! And so is this. Questions? Nope.");
```

```
Excitement: This is a sentence
Boring: And so is this
Question: Questions
Boring: Nope
```

---

hasmatch

```
"string" hasmatch 'pattern'
```

Determine if the string contains a substring that matches the specified pattern. Subsequent calls to this predicate with the same string, pattern combination will check if there is another pattern beyond the first one.

Parameters

`"string"` - the string to check

`'pattern'` - a regular expression pattern that defines a substring to match for

- 6. Regular Epxressions - tutorial on regular expression language

---

indexOf

```
$ indexOf("string", "substr", [start])
```

Returns the index of "substr" inside of "string" starting at the specified start index.

Parameters

`"string"` - the string to search.

`"substr"` - the substring to search for.

`start` - the position from which to begin the search (default is 0)

Example

```
$string = "this is a test";

$start = 0;
while $index (indexOf($string, " ", $start))
{
   println("$start $+ : $+ $index " . substr($string, $start, $index));
   $start = $index + 1;
}

println("$start $+ :end " . substr($string, $start));
```

```
0:4 this
5:7 is
8:9 a
10:end test
```

---

ismatch

`"string" ismatch 'pattern'`

Determine if the string matches the specified pattern.

Parameters

`"string"` - the string to check

`'pattern'` - a regular expression pattern that defines a substring to match for

- 6. Regular Epxressions - tutorial on regular expression language

---

iswm

`? '*filter*' iswm "string"`

Determine if the specified wildcard pattern is a match to the string.

Parameters

`'*filter*'` - a wildcard pattern.The following table provides a refresher of the wildcard matching meta characters.

Meta character	Meaning
*	Matches any zero or more characters (non-greedy*)
**	Matches any zero or more characters (greedy*)
?	Matches a single character
\	Escapes a wildcard character i.e. *

A greedy matcher will try to consume as many characters as possible before continuing to the next part of the wildcard string.

`"string"` - the string to check

Example

```
@strings = @("test", "task", "turf", "tusk", "dusk",
             "musk", "tease", "torso", "stochastic");

foreach $var (@strings) {
   if ('t*s*' iswm $var) {
      println($var);
   }
}
```

```
test
task
tusk
tease
torso
```

---

join

```
$ join("string", @array|&closure)
```

joins the elements of @array with "string"

Parameters

`"string"` - the delimeter to join the elements together with.

`@array` - an array of elements to join together

`&closure` - a generator function to create elements to join with the specified string

---

lc

```
$ lc("STRiNG")
```

Returns a lowercase version of the specified string

Parameters

`"STRiNG" - the string to lowercase.-`

---

left

```
$ left("string", n)
```

Returns the left n characters of "string"

Parameters

`"string"` - the string to get the characters from.

`n` - number of characters to grab

---

lindexOf

```
$ lindexOf("string", "substr", [start])
```

Returns the last index of "substr" inside of "string" counting backwards from the specified start index.

Parameters

`"string"` - the string to search.

`"substr"` - the substring to search for.

`start` - the position from which to begin the search (default is the end of the string)

matched

```
@ matched()
```

returns the matches from a "string" applied to a regex 'pattern' during an `ismatch/hasmatch` check

matches

```
@ matches("string", 'pattern', [n], [m])
```

returns the matches from "string" applied to the regex 'pattern'. if n is specified this will return the grouped matches of the n'th substring matching the specified pattern. if n and m are specified, all of the grouped matches of the n-m substrings will be returned.

Parameters

`"string"` - the string to match against the pattern and extract substrings from

`'pattern'` - a regular expression pattern that defines wether or not we have a match

- 6. Regular Epxressions - tutorial on regular expression language

mid

```
$ mid("string", start, [length])
```

Returns a substring of the specified "string" starting from the start index followed by the next n chars

Parameters

`"string"` - the string to grab a substring of.

`start` - the start index. (defaults to 0)

`length` - number of characters to grab starting at the start index.

pack

```
$ pack('format', $x, ...)
```

packs data into a string of bytes. each format character corresponds to one or more arguments.

```
$ pack('format', @array)
```

packs data into a string of bytes. each format character corresponds to one or more array elements.

Parameters

`'format'` - a string describing the number of values to expect and their types.

- 8.3 Binary I/O - summary of pack/unpack template characters

`$x, ...` - an arbitrary piece of data. the pack format describes how many pieces of data to expect and what type to pack them into.

`@array` - an array full of arbitrary pieces of data used by this function.

---

replace

```
$ replace("string", 'pattern', "new", [n])
```

Replaces each substring of the specified string that matches the regular expression pattern with the specified new string.

Parameters

`"string"` - the string to replace text in.

`'pattern'` - a regular expression pattern defining a substring that should be replaced.

- 6. Regular Epxressions - tutorial on regular expression language

`"new"` - the new text to replace each occurence of the pattern with. Within this string the literals $1, $2, etc. will be expanded to the pattern groupings captured by the pattern matcher. These are not Sleep variables, rather they are a special sequence interpreted by the regex engine.

`n` - if specified, only n occurences will be replaced. The default is to replace all matching substrings.

replaceAt

```
$ replaceAt("string", "new", index, [n])
```

Replaces n characters starting at the specified index with the new string.

Parameters

`"string"` - the string to replace text in.

`"new"` - the new string to insert into the "string".

`index` - the index to insert the new string into

`n` - number of characters to remove starting at the index (defaults to length of "new")

Example

```
$string = "this is a test, really";
$string = replaceAt($string, "drill", 10, 4);

println($string);
```

this is a drill, really

right

```
$ right("string", n)
```

Returns the right n characters of "string"

Parameters

`"string"` - the string to get the characters from.

`n` - number of characters to grab

split

```
@ split('pattern', "string", [limit])
```

splits the specified string by the specified pattern

Parameters

`"string"` - the string to split

`'pattern'` - the pattern that defines substrings this string should be broken up by.

- 6. Regular Epxressions - tutorial on regular expression language

`limit` - limits the number of segments to split the sentence into.

---

strlen

```
$ strlen("string")
```

Returns the length of the specified string.

Parameters

`"string"` - the string to obtain the length of.

---

strrep

```
$ strrep("string", "old", "new", ...)
```

Replaces occurrences of old with new in string. accepts multiple old, new parameters.

Parameters

`"string"` - the string to replace text in.

`"old"` - the substring to search for and eliminate.

`"new"` - the new string to replace the old string with.

`...` - multiple pairs of "old", "new" strings can be specified saving multiple calls to this function.

---

substr

```
$ substr("string", start, [end])
```

Extracts a substring of the specified string from the specified start index up to but not including the specified end index.

Parameters

`"string"` - the string to grab a substring of.

`start` - the start index. (defaults to 0)

`end` - the optional end index, if not specified will default to pulling the rest of the string.

Example

```
$string = "abcdefghijklmnopqrstuvwxyz";
$substr = substr($string, 13, 18);

println($substr);
```

nopqr

---

tr

```
$ tr("string", "matcher", "replacement", ['options'])
```

A character translation utility similar to the UNIX tr command. A transliteration consists of a pattern of characters to match and a pattern, typically of equal length, of characters to replace each match with. The tr utility loops through a specified string character by character. Each character is compared against the pattern of matching characters. If the character matches one of the pattern characters it is either replaced with the replacement character mapped to that matcher or it is deleted. Which action is taken depends on what options are specified.

Parameters

`"string"` - the string to apply this translation function to.

`"matcher"` - the characters that will be swapped out. Ranges will be expanded to all of the characters. A range is specified as *n-m* where *n* is the starting character (A-Z, a-z, 0-9) and *m* is the ending character. Backwards ranges are allowed as well. The matcher pattern may also contain the following character classes:

Sequence	Meaning
.	Matches any character
\d	Matches any digit 0-9
\D	Matches any non-digit

Sequence	Meaning
\s	Matches any whitespace character
\S	Matches any non-whitespace character
\w	Matches any word character (a-z, A-Z, _, and 0-9)
\W	Matches any non-word character
\\	Matches a literal backslash
\.	Matches a literal period
\-	Matches a literal dash

`"replacement"` - a string of replacement characters that maps 1:1 (after expansion) to the "matcher" string. As with the "matcher" string, ranges are expanded here as well.

`'options'` - A combination of the following parameters that alters the behavior of the matcher/translator.

Sequence	Name	Description
c	complement	negates matcher pattern forcing matcher chars/patterns to match their complement.
d	delete	delete all characters with no mapping in the replacement pattern.
s	squeeze	squeeze together matches that occur next to eachother. Deletes repeated matches.

Example

```
# A simple ROT13 Translator (for extra security run it twice...)

$cipher = tr("sleep rocks", "a-z", "n-za-m");
$plain  = tr($cipher, "a-z", "n-za-m");

println("Cipher: $cipher   Plain: $plain");
```

Cipher: fyrrc ebpxf   Plain: sleep rocks

```
# remove all duplicate chars from $string

$string = "thhisss   iiiisss mmmy sssstrriinngg";
$string = tr($string, "a-zA-Z0-9 ", "a-zA-Z0-9 ", "sd");

println($string);
```

this is my string

---

uc

```
$ uc("string")
```

Returns a uppercase version of the specified string

Parameters

`"string" - the string to uppercase.-`

---

unpack

```
@ unpack('format', "string")
```

unpacks data from the specified sleep string. data is returned as a sleep array with each scalar set to a type as specified in the format string

Parameters

`'format'` - a string describing the number of packed values and their types.

- 8.3 Binary I/O - summary of pack/unpack template characters

`"string"` - a scalar string containing serialized data

Appendix H: Utility Functions

This appendix is a mixed bag of everything else. All of the functionality that didn't fit into the other categories is located here.

---

acquire

```
acquire($semaphore)
```

blocks the current thread of execution until the semaphore count is > 0, when that happens the semaphore count is decremented.

Parameters

`$semaphore` - the semaphore to check and decrement

---

casti

```
$ casti($scalar, 't')
```

casts an individual $scalar into an object scalar representing a Java value

Parameters

`$scalar` - the scalar to cast into a Java value

`'t'` - the type to cast to

Character	Description
b	byte
c	char
d	double
f	float
h	short
i	int
l	long
z	boolean
o	java.lang.Object
*	Java Object (determined by class of scalars object value)

Example

```
$cast = casti(1, 'b');
println([$cast getClass]);

$cast = casti(33.5, 'f');
println([$cast getClass]);
```

class java.lang.Byte
class java.lang.Float

checkError

```
$ checkError([$error])
```

Returns the last error message to occur.

Parameters

`$error` - a scalar to place the last error object into. Often times this error object will be an instance of a `java.lang.Exception`.

compile_closure

```
& compile_closure("code", ...)
```

Creates a new Sleep closure from the specified string of Sleep code.

Parameters

"code" - a string containing the statements of the function.

... - a series of key/value pairs to be installed into the closure environment.

Example

```
$foo = compile_closure('return $1 * $x;', $x => 5);
println("\$foo is $foo");
println('[$foo: 2]   - ' . [$foo: 2]);
println('[$foo: 8]   - ' . [$foo: 8]);
println('[$foo: 4.3] - ' . [$foo: 4.3]);
```

```
$foo is &closure[eval:0]#707
[$foo: 2]   - 10
[$foo: 8]   - 40
[$foo: 4.3] - 21.5
```

---

copy

`@ copy(@array)`

Returns a shallow copy of the specified array.

`$ copy($scalar)`

Returns a shallow copy of the specified scalar.

`% copy(%hash)`

Returns a shallow copy of the specified hash.

Parameters

`@array|$scalar|%hash` - the data to copy.

---

debug

`$ debug([level])`

query/set the debug level for the current script environment.

Parameters

`level` - an integer specifying the current debug level. Debug levels can be OR'd together.The following debug levels can be combined with the OR operator i.e. `1 | 24`:

Level	Description
1	display all hard errors as runtime warnings.
2	display all soft errors as runtime warnings. These are the same errors that are caught programatically using `&checkError`
4	display a runtime warning for the first time use of non-declared variables.
8	trace all function calls (collects profiler statistics)
24	trace function calls only for the purpose of collecting profiler statistics
34	"throw" all errors flagged for use with `&checkError`
64	trace all predicate decisions (follow program logic)
128	trace propagation of tainted values

If no argument is specified then the current debug level is returned with no changes.

---

eval

```
$ eval("code")
```

Parses and evaluates the specified sleep code returning the value of the code.

Parameters

`"code"` - a string containing the statements to evaluate.

---

exit

```
exit(["reason"])
```

Causes the currently executing script to stop executing.

Parameters

`"reason"` - an optional parameter, when a reason is specified, this will be printed as a runtime warning.

expr

```
$ expr("expr")
```

Parses and evaluates the specified sleep expression code returning the value of the expression.

Parameters

`"expr"` - a string containing the expression to evaluate.

Example

```
$value  = expr('3 * 10 + sqrt(144)');
println($value);
```

42.0

function

```
& function('&name')
```

Obtains a reference to the specified function.

Parameters

`'&name'` - the name of the function to obtain the handle for.

getStackTrace

```
@ getStackTrace()
```

Within the context of a catch block, this function will return a trace of the Sleep call stack that caused the caught exception condition to occur. Returns an empty array otherwise.

global

```
global('$x $y')
```

Parses the specified string and declares all variables in the string as global variables.

Parameters

`'$x $y' - a string containing variable names separated by spaces.-`

---

iff

```
$ iff(comparison, [$iftrue], [$iffalse])
```

Takes a comparison as the first parameter and returns it's second parameter if and only if the condition is true. The third parameter is returned if and only if the condition is false.

Parameters

`comparison` - a condition to check for i.e. `$x > 0`

`$iftrue` - a value to return if the comparison evaluates to true. defaults to scalar integer 1.

`$iffalse` - a value to return if the comparison evaluates to false. defaults to *$null*

---

include

```
use(['/path/to/file.jar'], 'script.sl')
```

Compiles and executes the specified script in the current script context.

Parameters

`'/path/to/file.jar'` - optionally a jar file that contains the script can be specified. If no .jar file is specified then the script will be loaded from the sleep.classpath value.

`'script.sl'` - this is the script to load and execute within the current script environment.

Example

```
# foo.sl:
# sub foo {
#   println("Hello World! Hello $name");
# }

include("foo.sl");
```

```
$name = "Horatio";
foo();
```

Hello World! Hello Horatio

inline

`inline(&closure)`

Dynamically invokes the specified closure as if it was an inline function occuring within the local scope.

Parameters

`&closure` - the closure to invoke.

Example

```
inline form
{
   println('<form action="'.$1.'">');
   inline($2);
   println('  <input type="submit" value="Submit to '.$title.'">');
   println('</form>');
}

inline select
{
   println('  <select name="'.$1.'">');
   foreach $item ($2)
   {
      println('    <option>'.$item.'</option>');
   }
   println('  </select>');
}

sub buildPage
{
   local('$title');
   $title = "My Website!!";

   form("favorites",
   {
      println('<br>Colors? ');
      select('colors', @("#FF0000", "#00FF00", "#0000FF"));
   });
```

```
}

buildPage();
```

<form action="favorites">

Colors?
<select name="colors">
<option>#FF0000</option>
<option>#00FF00</option>
<option>#0000FF</option>
</select>
<input type="submit" value="Submit to My Website!!">
</form>

---

invoke

```
$ invoke(&closure, @args, ["message"], [key => value, ...])
```

Dynamically invokes the specified closure. Allows programatic specification of arguments, key/value pairs, and the message parameter.

Parameters

`&closure` - the closure to invoke.

`@args` - an array to use as the argument source to pass to the closure.

`"message"` - the $0 i.e. message parameter for the closure.

`key => value` - an option to set against the invoked function.

> `$this => &closure2` - if a $this is specified, then the closure invocation will use the this scope of &closure2
>
> `parameters => %hash` - if the parameters key is specified, then the right hand side hash will be used as the source of all named arguments passed to the &closure.

Example

```
sub foo {
   println("Hello: $name $+ , I got your message $0");
   println("The sum of $1 + $2 is: " . ($1 + $2));
}
```

```
invoke(&foo, @(3, 45), "call mother",
              parameters => %($name => "Raffi"));
```

Hello: Raffi, I got your message call mother
The sum of 3 + 45 is: 48

---

is

```
? $a is $b
```

Determine if *$a* references the same data as *$b*

Parameters

`$a` - any scalar

`$b` - any scalar

---

isa

```
? $a isa ^Class
```

Determine if object value of *$a* is an instance of the specified `^Class`

Parameters

`$a` - any scalar

`^Class` - a class to check.

---

lambda

```
& lambda(&closure, [$key => "value", ...])
```

Copies *&closure* into a new closure. The new closure environment is initialized with all of the specified key/value pair arguments.

Parameters

`&closure` - the closure to copy into a new instance.

`$key => value` - sets `$key` in the this scope of the new closure to the right hand side value.!!this-

`...` - any number of `$key => value` pairs may be specified.

---

let

```
& let(&closure, $key => "value", ...)
```

Updates the specified closure's environment with all of the key/value pair arguments. Returns the specified closure.

Parameters

`&closure` - the closure to update the "this" scope for.

`$key => value` - sets $key in the this scope of the specified closure to the right hand side value.

> `$this => &closure2` - if a *$this* is specified, then the resulting closure will share its this scope with *&closure2*

Example

```
$foo = { println("My favorite is $icecream with $topping"); };
let($foo, $icecream => "mint chocolate chip",
          $topping => "sprinkles");
[$foo];
let($foo, $topping => "strawberries"); # update $foo with a new $topping
[$foo];
```

```
My favorite is mint chocolate chip with sprinkles
My favorite is mint chocolate chip with strawberries
```

---

local

```
local('$x $y')
```

Parses the specified string and declares all variables in the string as local variables.

Parameters

`'$x $y'` - a string containing variable names separated by spaces.

newInstance

```
$ newInstance(^Class|@array, &closure)
```

Creates an instance of the specified Java interface (or interfaces if an array is used) backed by the specified closure.

Parameters

`^Class` - the class to create an instance of (limited to Java interfaces for now)

`@array` - an array of Java classes to create an instance of

`&closure` - the closure to back this proxy Java object with.

Example

```
@list = @("a", "b", "c", "d", "e");

sub iterator
{
   if ($0 eq "hasNext")
   {
      return size(@data);
   }

   if ($0 eq "next")
   {
      return shift(@data);
   }
}

$iter = newInstance(^java.util.Iterator, lambda(&iterator, @data =>
@list));

while ([$iter hasNext])
{
   $element = [$iter next];
   println($element);
}
```

```
a
b
c
d
e
```

popl

```
popl([$var => value, ...])
```

removes current local scope restoring previous scope.

Parameters

`[$var => $value, ...]` - the restored local scope may be updated with these key/value pairs taken from the current scope.

profile

```
@ profile()
```

Returns the profiler statistics for the current script environment. Profiler statistics will only be collected if DEBUG_TRACE_CALLS (8) or DEBUG_TRACE_PROFILE_ONLY (24) are enabled.

pushl

```
pushl([$var => value, ...])
```

creates an additional local scope.

Parameters

`[$var => $value, ...]` - the local scope may be initialized with these key/value pairs.

release

```
release($semaphore)
```

increments the count value of the specified semaphore. notifies other threads waiting on this semaphore

Parameters

`$semaphore` - the semaphore to increment

scalar

```
$ scalar($object)
```

Runs the specified object through the Java type to Sleep scalar conversion process. This same process used by HOES.

Parameters

`$object` - an object scalar

Example

```
println("Pre Conversion---");

$bytes = cast("this is a string", "b");
println("Class: " . [$bytes getClass]);
println("Type:  " . typeOf($bytes));

println("Post Conversion---");

$value = scalar($bytes);
println("Class: " . [$value getClass]);
println("Type:  " . typeOf($value));
```

```
Pre Conversion---
Class: class [B
Type:  class sleep.engine.types.ObjectValue
Post Conversion---
Class: class java.lang.String
Type:  class sleep.engine.types.StringValue
```

semaphore

```
$ semaphore(initial_count)
```

Creates a counting semaphore suitable for use with acquire and release. A semaphore is a synchronization primitive used to protect critical sections of code.

Parameters

`initial_count` - the initial value of the semaphore. Default value is 1 (a binary semaphore).

Example

```
%shared = %(produce => semaphore(0),
            consume => semaphore(1),
            buffer  => $null);

sub producer
{
   for ($x = 0; $x < 3; $x++)
   {
      acquire(%shared["consume"]);
      println("Produce: $x * 3");
      %shared["buffer"] = $x * 3;
      release(%shared["produce"]);
   }
}

sub consumer
{
   for ($y = 0; $y < 3; $y++)
   {
      acquire(%shared["produce"]);
      println("Consume: " . %shared["buffer"]);
      release(%shared["consume"]);
   }
}

fork(&consumer, \%shared);
fork(&producer, \%shared);
```

```
Produce: 0 * 3
Consume: 0
Produce: 1 * 3
Consume: 3
Produce: 2 * 3
Consume: 6
```

---

setf

```
setf('&function', &closure)
```

Binds a closure to the specified function name.

Parameters

`'&function'` - a string consisting of a function name to bind the closure to.

`&closure` - the closure to bind to the specified function name. A value of $null will remove the function binding.

---

setField

```
setField(^Class|$object, field => value, ...)
```

Sets any number of public/protected fields of the specified class or instance of $object to their corresponding values.

Parameters

`^Class` - a literal of the class to set a static field for.

`$object` - an instance of a class to set a field for.

`field => value` - an arbitrary field name followed by a corresponding value which is converted to the type Java expects.

`...` - the field => value parameter can be repeated any number of times with more values to set.

---

sleep

```
sleep(n)
```

Blocking call that forces the current executing thread to sleep for n milliseconds

Parameters

`n` - number of milliseconds to sleep for.

---

systemProperties

```
% systemProperties()
```

Returns a hash of the available system properties.

Example

```
# set a system property
```

```
[System setProperty: "test.prop", "foo"];

# retreive it:

println(systemProperties()["test.prop"]);
```

foo

---

taint

```
$ taint($scalar)
```

Taints the specified scalar

Parameters

`$scalar` - the scalar to taint

---

this

```
this('$x $y')
```

Parses the specified string and declares all variables in the string as variables specific to the scope of the current closure.

Parameters

`'$x $y'` - a string containing variable names separated by spaces.

Example

```
global('$x');

sub foo {
   this('$x');
   $x = $x + 1;
   println("&foo: \$x is $x");
}

$x = "bar!";
foo();
println("global: \$x is $x");
foo();
foo();
```

```
&foo: $x is 1
global: $x is bar!
&foo: $x is 2
&foo: $x is 3
```

---

typeOf

`^ typeOf($scalar)`

Returns the Java class of the container referenced by *$scalar*

Parameters

`$scalar` - The scalar to return the type of

---

untaint

`$ untaint($scalar)`

Untaints the specified scalar

Parameters

`$scalar` - the scalar to untaint

Example

```
# makes user input safe for use within a regex pattern
# we use inline because all function return values are considered
# tainted if an arg is tainted.  inline allows us to abstract our
# operation on the argument and untaint the value.
inline quote_regex
{
   untaint($1);
   $1 = "\\Q $+ $1 $+ \\E";
}

println("before: " . iff(-istainted @ARGV[0], "tainted!", "not
tainted"));
quote_regex(@ARGV[0]);

println("after: " . iff(-istainted @ARGV[0], "tainted!", "not tainted"));
println(@ARGV[0]);
```

```
$ java -Dsleep.taint=true -jar sleep.jar untaint.sl ".*?"
before: tainted!
after: not tainted
\Q.*?\E
```

---

use

```
use(^Class)
```

Installs the specified class (which is a *sleep.interfaces.Loadable*) into the current Sleep environment. This is a way of extending the Sleep language at runtime.

```
use(['/path/to/file.jar'], 'Loadable')
```

Dynamically loads a specified Sleep bridge and installs it into the current Sleep environment. This is a way of extending the Sleep language at runtime with Sleep bridges.

Parameters

`^Class` - the class to instantiate a new instance of and install into the current Sleep environment

`'/path/to/file.jar'` - optionally a jar file that contains the bridge classes can be specified. If no .jar file is specified then the bridge will be loaded from the sleep.classpath value.

`'Loadable'` - this is the fully qualified package+class name of the bridge class that implements sleep.interfaces.Loadable. This class will be dynamically instantiated and its scriptLoaded method will be called against the current script environment.

Example

```
# This example shows how to connect to a MySQL database and
# execute a simple query with Slumber by Andreas Ravnestad

import no.printf.slumber.JDBC from: slumber.jar;

use(^JDBC);

$handle = dbConnect('com.mysql.jdbc.Driver',
          'jdbc:mysql://localhost/database',
          'user', 'pass');

$result = dbQuery($handle, 'select * from table');
```

```
while (dbAssign($result, %row))
{
    println(%row);
}
```

---

warn

```
warn("text")
```

Prints "text" to the registered runtime warning watcher. Provides an application neutral way to print messages to the Sleep console.

Parameters

`"text"` - the text to write

---

watch

```
watch('$var @ar')
```

Declares all ovariables in the string as "watch" variables. Any attempt to set a value in a watched container will print out a warning. The warning does not prevent the setting of the variable. The value will change as normal.

Parameters

`'$var @ar'` - a string containing a space separated list of variables to watch. These vars must already exist.

About

The Sleep 2.1 manual was written during the Sleep development process. The print and online versions of this manual were generated from a custom markup using Sleep scripts. Diagrams were created with Omnigraffle on MacOS X. The print version was typeset with PrinceXML (http://www.princexml.com).

The cover image comes from a photo titled "Zonked" by Lynne Lancaster. The photo was modified with the GIMP using the oilify filter. The photo is used in compliance with the terms of the Image license agreement from sxc.hu.

The Author

Raphael Mudge is a former military scientist with a background in cyber operations. He has a formal education in Computer Science and holds a commission as a Captain in the US Air Force Reserve.

www.ingramcontent.com/pod-product-compliance
Lightning Source LLC
Chambersburg PA
CBHW080402060326
40689CB00019B/4104

* 9 7 8 1 4 3 8 2 2 7 2 3 8 *